13+ Maths

For the Common Entrance exams

The 13+ Maths exams can be tricky, but there's no need to panic — this brilliant CGP book has everything you need for exam success.

It's crammed full of crystal-clear study notes and step-by-step worked examples to help you understand every topic — for both the Core and Additional papers.

We've also included loads of practice questions to get you ready for the real thing, with fully worked answers at the back. So whichever papers you're taking, you'll be all set on exam day.

How to access your free Online Edition

This book includes a free Online Edition to read on your PC, Mac or tablet. You'll just need to go to **cgpbooks.co.uk/extras** and enter this code:

1059 7350 8874 8392

By the way, this code only works for one person. If somebody else has used this book before you, they might have already claimed the Online Edition.

Revision Guide

Contents

Section 1 — Numbers

Section 2 — Algebra

Section 3 — Graphs

Section 4 — Ratio, Proportion and Rates of Change

Section 5 — Geometry and Measures

Section 6 — Probability and Statistics

Published by CGP

Written by Richard Parsons.

Editors:
Emily Garrett, Sarah George, Georgina Paxman, Ben Train

With thanks to Shaun Harrogate and Lauren McNaughten for the proofreading.

With thanks to Jan Greenway for the copyright research.

ISBN: 978 1 78908 797 0

Printed by Elanders Ltd, Newcastle upon Tyne.
Clipart from Corel®

13+ Maths

If you're reading this, then chances are you're going to be tested on 13+ Maths at some point. At least this page should shed some light on what to expect come exam day...

There are **Three Papers** that Test the **Core Content**

1) For 13+ Maths you'll sit a <u>calculator</u> paper, a <u>non-calculator</u> paper and a <u>mental arithmetic</u> test.

2) These papers test the <u>Core content</u>.

You may be sitting the Foundation papers instead — these test the same material as the Core content, but the papers are easier.

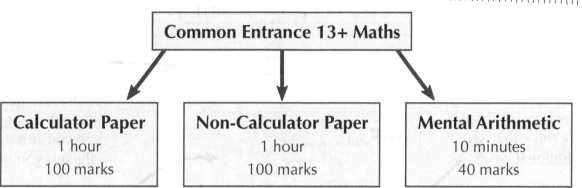

Common Entrance 13+ Maths

Calculator Paper	**Non-Calculator Paper**	**Mental Arithmetic**
1 hour	1 hour	10 minutes
100 marks	100 marks	40 marks

There's an **Extra Paper** for **Additional Content**

If you're not sure whether you're doing Additional or not, ask your teacher.

1) You <u>might</u> be entered for the <u>Additional paper</u>. If you are, you'll have to sit this <u>as well as</u> the three Core papers.

2) If you're sitting the Additional paper, you'll need to study the <u>Additional content</u> as well as the Core content — the Additional content covers topics that are <u>slightly harder</u> than the topics in the Core content.

3) The Additional paper is <u>1 hour</u> long, and is out of <u>100 marks</u>.

4) This paper is <u>more challenging</u> than the Core papers, so you might not be able to answer all the questions. It's <u>better</u> to give complete solutions to <u>some</u> questions instead of lots of <u>partial</u> solutions.

It's **Important** to Always **Show Your Working**

1) In all of the papers apart from the mental arithmetic test, you can <u>pick up marks</u> for showing the correct <u>working</u>.

2) That means even if you make a <u>mistake</u> with the final answer, you <u>won't lose</u> all of the marks for that question.

3) It also means that if you <u>don't</u> show your working you could <u>miss out</u> on marks, even if your final answer is <u>correct</u>.

4) Make sure your working is always <u>clear</u> and <u>easy to read</u>, and you write down <u>every step</u> that you take. Even if you use a <u>calculator</u>, write down <u>each stage</u> of the calculation.

5) Don't forget to <u>give units</u> in your answer if your answer has them — you'll <u>lose marks</u> for not including them.

How to Use This Book

Have a look at the following information — it'll explain what everything in this book means.

What You Need to **Learn** Depends on **Which Papers** you Sit

1) If you're only sitting the Core or Foundation papers, you'll need to learn everything in this book, apart from the content marked up with an Additional bar.

2) If you're also sitting the Additional paper, you'll need to learn everything in this book, including the content marked up with an Additional bar.

There Are Lots of **Features** to **Help** You **Learn**

Additional bars tell you if the content is for Additional students only. These bars will either say 'Additional' or 'A'.

At the bottom of every page, you'll find a box with some practice questions testing the content.

Additional bars on questions mean the questions are testing Additional content.

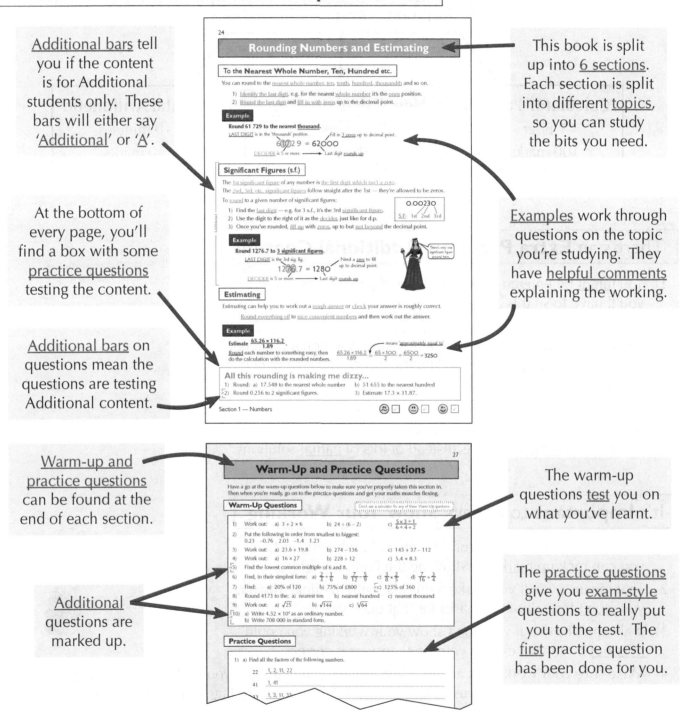

This book is split up into 6 sections. Each section is split into different topics, so you can study the bits you need.

Examples work through questions on the topic you're studying. They have helpful comments explaining the working.

Warm-up and practice questions can be found at the end of each section.

Additional questions are marked up.

The warm-up questions test you on what you've learnt.

The practice questions give you exam-style questions to really put you to the test. The first practice question has been done for you.

There are also summary questions at the end of each section, a glossary (p.124) and an index (p.136).

Calculating Tips

Here are some nifty tips and tricks that you'll need before you get going.

BODMAS | Brackets, Other, Division, Multiplication, Addition, Subtraction

<u>BODMAS</u> tells you the <u>ORDER</u> in which operations should be done: work out <u>Brackets</u> first, then <u>Other</u> things like powers, then <u>Divide</u> / <u>Multiply</u> groups of numbers before <u>Adding</u> or <u>Subtracting</u> them.

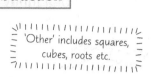 'Other' includes squares, cubes, roots etc.

Example

Work out $4 + 6 \div 2$.

1) Follow BODMAS — do the <u>division</u> first... $\quad 4 + 6 \div 2$
$\quad = 4 + 3$
2) ...then the <u>addition</u>: $\quad = 7$

Calculate $10 - 2^3$.

1) Start by working out the <u>cube</u>: $\quad 10 - 2^3$
$\quad = 10 - 8$
2) Then do the <u>subtraction</u>: $\quad = 2$

Example

Find $2^3 - 6 \times 4 + 9$.

1) Start by working out the <u>cube</u>: $\quad 2^3 - 6 \times 4 + 9$
2) And now the <u>multiplication</u>: $\quad = 8 - 6 \times 4 + 9$
3) Then do the subtraction and addition <u>in order</u> from <u>left to right</u>: $\quad = 8 - 24 + 9$
$\quad = -16 + 9 = -7$

If you don't follow the order of BODMAS, you get: $4 + 6 \div 2 = 10 \div 2 = 5$

Don't Be Scared of **Wordy Questions**

You'll probably come across some <u>wordy</u>, <u>real-life</u> questions in your exams and you'll have to work out what the question's asking you to do. Remember:

1) <u>READ</u> the question <u>carefully</u>. Work out <u>what bit of maths</u> you need to answer it.
2) <u>Underline</u> the <u>INFORMATION YOU NEED</u> to answer the question — you might not have to use <u>all</u> the numbers they give you.
3) Write out the question <u>IN MATHS</u> and answer it, showing all your <u>working</u> clearly.
4) You can <u>CHECK</u> your answers by seeing if they look <u>sensible</u>.

Example

Zahra's Clothing is having a <u>20% off</u> sale on all clothing items. A shirt originally cost <u>£25.</u> What is the price of the shirt <u>in the sale</u>?

The "<u>20% off</u>" tells you this is a <u>percentage change</u> question (covered on page 68). You need <u>£25</u> (the original price) and <u>20% off</u> (the percentage). It doesn't matter what the shop is called or what the item is. You want to take 20% off £25, so: 20% of £25 = £5 £25 − £5 = **£20** <u>Check</u>: £20 is a bit less than £25, so that seems about right.

Don't forget the units in your final answer — this is a question about cost in pounds, so the units will be £.

Wordy questions? I thought this was Maths, not English...

It's really important to check your working on BODMAS questions.
1) Find the value of: a) $11 - 5 \times 2$ b) $12 + 8 \div 4$ c) $6 + 4 \times 2$
2) Find the value of: a) $3 \times 6 + 15 \div 5$ b) $(6 \times 3) \div 3^2$ c) $2^3 \div 4 + 1 \times 2$

Calculating Tips

Hidden Brackets in Fractions

This is a bit of a funny one — when you have a fraction with calculations on the top or bottom you have to imagine they're in brackets and do them first.

Example

Work out $\dfrac{20 \times 5}{4 + 2 \times 3}$.

1) Imagine the top and bottom are both in brackets.

2) Now follow BODMAS to do the calculation.

$$\frac{(20 \times 5)}{(4 + 2 \times 3)}$$

$$= \frac{100}{(4 + 6)} = \frac{100}{10} = 10$$

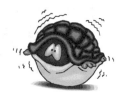

Calculators

Your calculator might be different to this one — so work out how to do everything on yours.

Make sure you know the important features on your calculator and how to use them.

Shift (or 2nd Func)

Press this first if you want to use something written above a button (e.g. the pi (π) above the ×10ˣ button).

Powers and Roots

E.g. 4 x^2 gives 4 squared = 16

2 $x^■$ 5 gives 2 to the power 5 = 32

And √ 25 gives the square root of 25 = 5

Fractions

E.g. for $\frac{1}{4}$, press 1 ▭ 4.
(If you have a button that looks like a^b_c instead, use it in the same way.) For $1\frac{3}{5}$, press

1 ▭ 3 ▭ 5 (you might have to press shift first).

To cancel down a fraction, enter it and press =.

Pressing the ▭ or S⇔D button also switches an answer between a fraction and a decimal.

3.6

The Answer

Before you jot down 3.6, think about what it means. E.g. in a money question, it might mean £3.60.

Brackets

Calculators use BODMAS (see page 3), so if there's part of a question you want the calculator to do FIRST then put brackets in to tell it so.

Memory (STO, RCL & M+)

E.g. for $\frac{840}{12 \times 8}$: Press 12 × 8 = and then STO M+ to store the bottom line in the memory. Then press 840 ÷ RCL M+ =, and the answer is **8.75**.

The 'Ans' button gives the number you got when you last pressed the '=' button.

Pi (π)

(See page 86 for more on π.)

The calculator stores the number for pi (= 3.141...). If it's above another button as shown here, press the shift button first.

Make sure you know how your calculator works...

1) Work out $\dfrac{20 \times 8}{4 + 4 \times 3}$ using hidden brackets and BODMAS. Then try it on your calculator.

Calculating Tips

Each time you see the word 'inverse', think 'opposite' — then make sure you know how they work.

Using Inverse Operations

Adding and Subtracting

Adding and subtracting are inverse operations. Start off with a number, add any number to it and then subtract the same number — you'll be back to the number you started with. You can use inverse operations to check your answers.

Example

Simon has 26p and steals 14p from his sister Emma. How much money does Simon have now?

Add the two amounts together to get the total.

$26 + 14 = 40p$

Check your answer by using the inverse operation — you should get the amount you started with.

$40 - 14 = 26p$ ✓

Multiplying and Dividing

Multiplying and dividing are inverse operations too. Start off with a number, multiply it by any number and then divide by the same number — you'll be back to the number you started with.

Example

Michelle has 3 bags each containing 4 coconuts. She empties all of the coconuts into a box. How many coconuts are in the box?

Multiply the two numbers together to get the total.

$3 \times 4 = 12$ coconuts

Check your answer by using the inverse operation — you should get the number of bags you started with.

$12 \div 4 = 3$ bags ✓

Division by Factors

Dividing by bigger numbers without a calculator can be a bit tricky. But if you break down the divisor (the number you're dividing by) into factors, it'll make life much easier.

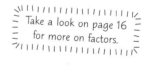
Take a look on page 16 for more on factors.

Example

It doesn't matter what order you divide in — but it's a good idea to start with the easiest one.

Work out 260 ÷ 20.

1) Write 20 as the product of two smaller numbers (factors).

$20 = 10 \times 2$

2) Divide 260 by 10...

$260 \div 10 \div 2$

3) ...and then by 2.

$= 26 \div 2 = 13$

Calculate 105 ÷ 15.

1) Rewrite 15 as two smaller factors.

$15 = 5 \times 3$

2) Now divide by 5...

$105 \div 5 \div 3$

3) ...and then by 3.

$= 21 \div 3 = 7$

Checking your answers can save you precious marks...

1) Use inverse operations to check your answers to the questions below.

   a) $34 + 16$ b) $108 - 59$ c) 23×7 d) $156 \div 6$

2) Use division by factors to work out the following: a) $350 \div 70$ b) $80 \div 16$

Place Value

You can use columns to work out the value of each digit in a big number or decimal.

Split **Big Numbers** into **Columns** and **Parts**

First, you need to know the <u>names</u> of all the <u>columns</u>. E.g. for the number <u>3 232 594</u>:

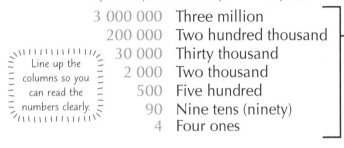

MILLIONS	HUNDRED-THOUSANDS	TEN-THOUSANDS	THOUSANDS	HUNDREDS	TENS	ONES
3	2	3	2	5	9	4

You can then <u>split any number up</u> into its <u>parts</u>, like this:

Line up the columns so you can read the numbers clearly.

3 000 000	Three million
200 000	Two hundred thousand
30 000	Thirty thousand
2 000	Two thousand
500	Five hundred
90	Nine tens (ninety)
4	Four ones

→ These add together to make <u>3 232 594</u>

You can also use the columns to work out the <u>value</u> of a certain digit.

E.g. In 3 232 <u>5</u>94, the value of the <u>5</u> is <u>5 hundreds</u>.

Look at **Big Numbers** in Groups of **Three**

To <u>read</u> or <u>write</u> a <u>BIG number</u>, follow these <u>steps</u>:

1) Start from the <u>right-hand side</u> of the number →.

2) Moving <u>left</u>, ←, put a space <u>every 3 digits</u> to break it up into <u>groups of 3</u>

3) Now going <u>right</u>, →, <u>read each group of three</u> as a separate number, as shown.

3,232,594

MILLIONS   THOUSANDS   The rest

So read as: 3 million, 232 thousand, 594
or write fully in words:
Three million, two hundred and thirty-two thousand, five hundred and ninety-four.

Split **Decimals** into **Decimal Places**

The <u>decimal places</u> have <u>names</u> too. E.g. for the number <u>173.753</u>:

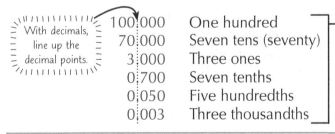

HUNDREDS	TENS	ONES	DECIMAL POINT	TENTHS	HUNDREDTHS	THOUSANDTHS
1	7	3	.	7	5	3

You can <u>split up decimals</u> into <u>parts</u> too:

With decimals, line up the decimal points.

100.000	One hundred
70.000	Seven tens (seventy)
3.000	Three ones
0.700	Seven tenths
0.050	Five hundredths
0.003	Three thousandths

→ These add together to make <u>173.753</u>

You can work out the <u>value</u> of a certain digit.

E.g. In 173.7<u>5</u>3, the value of the <u>5</u> is <u>5 hundredths</u>.

Baking with hundredths and thousandths is a lot less fun...

1) Write these numbers out fully in words: a) 9 905 285   b) 6 054 203

2) Write down in words: a) the value of the 6 in 0.684   b) the value of the 7 in 4.357

Ordering Numbers

Here's a page filled with easy examples — it's all about ordering numbers.

Ordering **Whole Numbers**

Ascending order means smallest to largest.
Descending order means largest to smallest.

Example

Write these numbers in ascending order: –53   53   17   2321   –754   421   548   –88   1729

1)   First put them into groups with the <u>negative ones first</u>:

negative	2-digit	3-digit	4-digit
–53 –754 –88	53 17	421 548	2321 1729

2)   Then just put each separate group in <u>order of size</u> from smallest to largest.

    –754   –88   –53   17   53   421   548   1729   2321

Ordering **Decimals**

You can also use number lines for ordering numbers.

1)   Do the <u>whole number bit first</u>, then the bit <u>after the decimal point</u>.

2)   If two numbers have the <u>same whole number</u> bit, order them by the <u>next digit</u>, etc.

Example

Write these numbers in order, from smallest to largest:
0.62   18.42   0.062   0.58   0.006   18.56   8.4

1)   First order them by the <u>whole number</u> bit from <u>smallest</u> to <u>largest</u>.

    0.62   0.062   0.58   0.006   8.4   18.42   18.56

2)   Now order each whole number group by the first number <u>after the decimal point</u> from smallest to largest.

    (0.062   0.006   0.58   0.62) (8.4) (18.42   18.56)

3)   0.062 and 0.006 have the <u>same first number</u> after the decimal point, so keep going and compare their <u>second numbers</u>. Order them by size.

    (0.006   0.062) 0.58   0.62   8.4   18.42   18.56

Greater Than and **Less Than**

These <u>symbols</u> are used to show if something is <u>bigger</u> (or <u>smaller</u>) than <u>something else</u>.

Symbol	Meaning
>	Greater than
<	Less than
≥	Greater than or equal to
≤	Less than or equal to

Example

Which of these statements is true?   a) 5 > 7   b) 6 < 9

a)   5 > 7 means 5 is <u>greater than</u> 7, which is false.
b)   6 < 9 means 6 is <u>less than</u> 9, which is true.

Additional

Is the following statement true? 2 ≥ 2
2 ≥ 2 means 2 is <u>greater than or equal to</u> 2 — they are both <u>equal</u> so this statement is true.

I tried to order numbers, but they just don't listen to me...

1)   Put these numbers in descending order: 35   318   –16   –24   107   –6   –5   –115
2)   Write > or < to complete the expressions: a) 30 000 ____ 29 950   b) 0.005 ____ 0.045

Addition and Subtraction

I'm sure you're all chomping at the bit to learn some methods of addition and subtraction.

Adding

1) Line up the <u>ones</u> columns of each number.
2) Add up the columns from <u>right to left</u>.
3) <u>Carry over</u> any spare tens to the next column.

Example

Add together 342, 231 and 78.

1)
```
  342     Line up
  231     ones.
+  78
    1
   1
```
2 + 1 + 8 = <u>11</u>
<u>Write</u> 1 and carry the 1.

2)
```
  342
  231
+  78
   51
  1 1
```
Remember to add the carried number too.
4 + 3 + 7 + 1 = <u>15</u>
<u>Write</u> 5 and carry the 1.

3)
```
  342
  231
+  78
  651
  1 1
```
3 + 2 + 1 = <u>6</u>
<u>Write</u> 6 and you're done.

Subtracting

1) Line up the <u>ones</u> columns of each number.
2) Working <u>right to left</u>, subtract the <u>bottom</u> number from the <u>top</u> number.
3) If the top number is <u>smaller</u> than the bottom number, <u>borrow</u> 10 from the left.

Example

Work out 372 − 324.

1)
```
   6 12
  3 7 2    Line up
 − 324     ones.
```
You can't do 2 − 4, so <u>borrow 10</u> from the left.

2)
```
   6 12
  3 7 2
 − 324
   0 4 8
```
12 − 4 = 8
6 − 2 = 4
3 − 3 = 0

And with **Decimals**...

The <u>method is just the same</u>, but start instead by lining up the <u>decimal points</u>.

Example

Work out 0.7 + 32.2 + 1.65.

1)
```
   0.70     Decimal points lined up.
  32.20     It often helps to write in
+  1.65     extra zeros to make all the
    .55     decimals the same length.
   1
```
7 + 2 + 6 = 15 — write 5 and carry the 1.

2)
```
   0.70
  32.20
+  1.65
  34.55
   1
```
0 + 2 + 1 + carried 1 = 4

Ben has £5 and spends 91p on a pie. How much does he have left?

1)
```
  £5.00     Decimal points lined up.
 −£0.91
```
0 is smaller than 1, so you can't do 0 − 1.

2)
```
   4 10
  £5.00     Borrow 10...
 −£0.91
```

3)
```
   4 10 10
  £5.00     ...then borrow 10 again.
 −£0.91
  £4.09
```
10 − 1 = 9
9 − 9 = 0
4 − 0 = 4

Carrying all these remainders is heavy going...

1) a) 113 + 645 + 39   b) 1239 − 387   c) 0.58 + 1.47 + 16.4
2) Rob beat his 100 m sprint time of 13.22 seconds by 0.87 seconds. What is his new best time?

Multiplying by 10, 100, etc.

This stuff is easy peasy — I'm sure you'll have no problem flying through this page.

1) To **Multiply** Any Number by **10**

Move all the digits <u>ONE</u> place <u>BIGGER</u>
and if it's needed, <u>ADD A ZERO</u> on the end.

E.g. $1.6 \times 10 = 1\ 6$

$6213 \times 10 = 6\ 2\ 1\ 3\ 0$

$672.12 \times 10 = 6\ 7\ 2\ 1\ .\ 2$

2) To **Multiply** Any Number by **100**

Move all the digits <u>TWO</u> places <u>BIGGER</u>
and <u>ADD ZEROS</u> if necessary.

Add zeros up to the decimal point.

E.g. $3.5 \times 100 = 3\ 5\ 0$

$78 \times 100 = 7\ 8\ 0\ 0$

$3.7734 \times 100 = 3\ 7\ 7\ .\ 3\ 4$

3) To **Multiply** by **1000**, the Same Rule Applies:

Move all the digits <u>THREE</u> places <u>BIGGER</u>
and <u>ADD ZEROS</u> if necessary.

You always <u>move</u> all the <u>DIGITS</u> this much:

<u>1 place for 10</u>,
<u>2 places for 100</u>,
<u>3 places for 1000</u>, etc.

The number of zeros tells you the number of places to move.

E.g. $99.67 \times 1000 = 9\ 9\ 6\ 7\ 0$

$8.4 \times 1000 = 8\ 4\ 0\ 0$

4) To **Multiply** by Numbers like **20, 300, 8000** etc.

<u>MULTIPLY</u> by <u>2</u> or <u>3</u> or <u>8</u> etc. <u>FIRST</u>,
then move all the digits so many places <u>BIGGER</u> (⟵)
according to how many zeros there are.

Example

Calculate 110 × 500.

1) First <u>multiply</u> by 5... $110 \times 5 = 550$
2) ...then move the digits <u>2 places bigger</u>. $550 \times 100 = \mathbf{55\ 000}$

Multiplying just got 100 times more exciting...

1) Work out: a) 6.4×10 b) 852×100 c) 0.0885×1000 d) 5.4×50 e) 3.2×600
2) A type of centipede has 200 legs. How many legs do 16 of these centipedes have altogether?

Dividing by 10, 100, etc.

This is pretty easy stuff too. Just make sure you know it — that's all.

1) To **Divide** Any Number by **10**

Move all the digits <u>ONE</u> place <u>SMALLER</u> and if it's needed, <u>REMOVE ZEROS</u> at the end of the decimal part.

E.g. $32.2 \div 10 = 3.22$

$6541 \div 10 = 654.1$

$4200 \div 10 = 420.\emptyset = 420$

2) To **Divide** Any Number by **100**

Move all the digits <u>TWO</u> places <u>SMALLER</u> and <u>REMOVE ANY ZEROS</u> at the end of the decimal part.

E.g. $333.8 \div 100 = 3.338$

$160 \div 100 = 1.6\emptyset = 1.6$

$1729 \div 100 = 17.29$

3) To **Divide** by **1000**, the Same Rule Applies:

Move all the digits <u>THREE</u> places <u>SMALLER</u> and <u>REMOVE ANY ZEROS</u> at the end of the decimal part.

You always <u>move</u> all the <u>DIGITS</u> this much:

<u>1 place for 10,</u>
<u>2 places for 100,</u>
<u>3 places for 1000,</u> etc.

The number of zeros tells you the number of places to move.

E.g. $6587 \div 1000 = 6.587$

$234 \div 1000 = 0.234$

4) To **Divide** by Numbers like **40, 300, 7000** etc.

<u>DIVIDE</u> by <u>4</u> or <u>3</u> or <u>7</u> etc. <u>FIRST</u>, then move all the digits so many places <u>SMALLER</u> (i.e. to the right ———▶) according to how many zeros there are.

Example

Calculate 180 ÷ 200.

1) First divide by 2... $180 \div 2 = 90$
2) ...then move the digits 2 places smaller. $90 \div 100 = 0.90 = 0.9$

Get rid of any extra zeros after the decimal point...

1) Work out: a) $8.59 \div 10$ b) $35698 \div 100$ c) $67.52 \div 1000$ d) $2080 \div 20$
2) Milly has 6798 shiny 1p coins. How much is this in pounds and pence?

Multiplying Without a Calculator

Multiplying with a calculator is a piece of cake. The real challenge is multiplying without one.

Multiplying by a One-Digit Number

Just follow these steps to multiply a big number by a one-digit number:

1) Write out the calculation with the big number on top and line up the place value columns.
2) Multiply the one-digit number by each part of the big number in turn.
   Start with the place value column of least value (it's always the one on the right).
3) Each time you get an answer of 10 or more, record the first digit of the answer below the next column (like you do when you're adding). You'll add this onto the next multiplication.

Example

Work out 327 × 3.

1) 3 2 7
 ×   3
    1       $7 \times 3 = 21$, so put a
    2   1 here and a 2 under
            the next column.

2) 3 2 7
 ×   3
   8 1 $2 \times 3 = 6$
    2   Add the extra
             2 to get 8.

3) 3 2 7
 ×   3
  9 8 1   Finish by
    2   multiplying
             3×3.

Multiplying by Bigger Numbers

There are lots of methods you can use for this. Two popular ones are shown below.

Example

Calculate 48 × 33.

The Traditional Method

Split it into separate multiplications, then add up the results in columns (from right to left).

```
      4 8
  ×   3 3
    1 4 4      This is 3 × 48.
  1 4 4 0      This is 30 × 48.
  1 5 8 4
               This is 144 + 1440.
```

The Grid Method

1) Split up each number into its ones and tens (and hundreds and thousands if it has them).

   48 = 40 + 8 and 33 = 30 + 3

2) Draw a grid, with the 'bits' of the numbers round the outside.

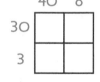

3) Multiply the bits round the edge to fill each square.

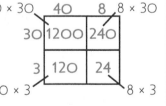

4) Finally, add up the numbers in the squares.

```
    1 2 0 0
      2 4 0
      1 2 0
  +     2 4
    1 5 8 4
```

Example

**Aston eats 16 almonds every day.
How many almonds will he eat in 132 days?**

```
    1 3 2
  ×   1 6
    7 9 2      This is 6 × 132.
  1 3 2 0      This is 10 × 132.
  2 1 1 2      This is 792 + 1320.
```

So Aston will eat **2112 almonds**.

Any method is fine, as long as the answer is right...

Two different multiplication methods — try them out on these questions to see which you prefer.
1) Work out   a) 472 × 8   b) 42 × 37   c) 509 × 64

Dividing Without a Calculator

OK, time for some dividing without a calculator — ready for another challenge?

Short Division

The Easy Case — Exact Division

When a division gives a <u>whole number</u> answer — it's pretty simple.

> You'll find it helpful to write out the first few multiples (see p.16) of the number you're dividing by.

Example

What is 848 ÷ 16?

1) Set out the division as shown. ——— $16\overline{)848}$

2) Look at the first digit under the line. 8 doesn't divide by 16, so <u>put a zero</u> above and look at the <u>next digit</u>. ——— $16\overline{)848}$ with **0**

3) $16 \times 5 = 80$, so 16 into 84 goes <u>5 times</u>, with a <u>remainder</u> of $84 - 80 = 4$. ——— carry the remainder

4) 16 into 48 goes <u>3 times exactly</u>. ——— the top line has the final answer

So **848 ÷ 16 = 53**

Multiples of 16:
$16 \times 1 = 16$
$16 \times 2 = 32$
$16 \times 3 = 48$
$16 \times 4 = 64$
$16 \times 5 = 80$

The Tricky Case — Non-Exact Division

When the division <u>doesn't</u> give a nice number, you can give your answer in <u>several</u> different ways.

Example

What is 658 ÷ 28?

1) Set out the division as shown. $28\overline{)658}$

2) 6 doesn't divide by 28, so <u>write a zero</u> above the 6 and look at the <u>next digit</u>. $28\overline{)658}$ with **023**

3) 28 into 65 goes <u>2 times</u> with a <u>remainder</u> of $65 - 56 = 9$, so put a <u>2</u> above the 5. ——— carry the remainder

4) 28 into 98 goes <u>3 times</u> with a remainder of $98 - 84 = 14$, so put a <u>3</u> above the 8 and remember the remainder of 14.

Multiples of 28:
$28 \times 1 = 28$
$28 \times 2 = 56$
$28 \times 3 = 84$
$28 \times 4 = 112$
$28 \times 5 = 140$

> Knowing the remainder is useful if you want to know how many of something is left after a division.

5) Now you can <u>either</u> give your answer as a <u>mixed fraction</u>, where the numerator is the <u>remainder</u> and the denominator is the <u>number you're dividing by</u>... <u>Either</u> $658 \div 28 = 23\frac{14}{28}$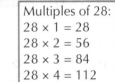

remainder / number you're dividing by

6) ...or keep going to give it as a <u>decimal</u>. Keep adding <u>zeros</u> after the decimal point and carry on. 28 goes into 140 exactly <u>5 times</u>, so you're done. <u>Or</u> **658 ÷ 28 = 23.5**

I won't be needing this any more — calc-u-later...

1) Work out   a) $128 \div 8$ b) $418 \div 19$ c) $550 \div 44$

2) Cyril shares 150 gummy worms equally among 12 friends. How many are left over?

Multiplying and Dividing with Decimals

On the last two pages you've seen how to multiply and divide whole numbers without a calculator. Well, decimals are the same if you just ignore the decimal points — worry about them at the end.

Multiplying Decimals

1) Start by <u>ignoring</u> the decimal points. Do the multiplication using <u>whole numbers</u>.
2) Count the <u>total</u> number of digits after the <u>decimal points</u> in the original numbers.
3) Make the answer have the <u>same number</u> of decimal places.

Example

Work out 4.8 × 1.64.

1) Do the <u>whole-number</u> multiplication: 48 × 164 = 7872
2) Count the digits <u>after</u> the decimal points: <u>4.8</u> × 1.<u>64</u> has <u>3 digits</u> after the decimal points — so will the answer.
3) Give the answer the <u>same number</u> of decimal places: 4.8 × 1.64 = **7.872**

Take a look at page 11 for multiplying whole numbers.

Dividing a **Decimal** by a **Whole Number**

For these, you just set the question out like a whole number division <u>but</u> put the <u>decimal point</u> in the answer <u>right above</u> the one in the question.

Example

What is 49.8 ÷ 6?

1) Put the <u>decimal point</u> in the answer above the one in the question.

            6 | 4 9 . 18   0 8 .3

2) 6 into 4 <u>doesn't go</u>, so <u>put a zero</u> above and look at the <u>next digit</u>.

3) 6 goes into 49 <u>8 times</u>, so carry the <u>remainder of 1</u>.

4) 6 goes into 18 <u>3 times exactly</u>. So 49.8 ÷ 6 = **8.3**

Dividing a **Number** by a **Decimal**

Two-for-one here — this works if you're dividing a whole number (or a decimal) by a decimal.

Example

What is 8.48 ÷ 0.16?

1) The trick here is to write it <u>as a fraction</u>: $8.48 \div 0.16 = \dfrac{8.48}{0.16}$
2) <u>Get rid of the decimals</u> by multiplying top and bottom by 100 (see p.9): $= \dfrac{848}{16}$
3) It's now a <u>decimal-free</u> division that you know how to solve: $= 53$ This is worked out on the previous page.

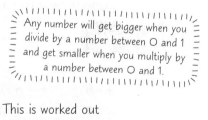

Any number will get bigger when you divide by a number between 0 and 1 and get smaller when you multiply by a number between 0 and 1.

Multiplying and dividing on one page — you're so lucky...

1) Work out: a) 2.87 × 42   b) 17.32 × 0.15   c) 5.1 ÷ 5
2) If one apple costs £0.32, how many apples can James buy with £20.48?
3) Work out 83.2 ÷ 0.13.

Negative Numbers

Numbers less than zero are negative. You can add, subtract, multiply and divide with them.

Adding and Subtracting with Negative Numbers

Use the <u>number line</u> for <u>addition</u> and <u>subtraction</u> involving negative numbers:

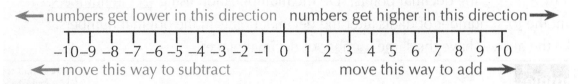

←numbers get lower in this direction numbers get higher in this direction→

–10 –9 –8 –7 –6 –5 –4 –3 –2 –1 0 1 2 3 4 5 6 7 8 9 10

←move this way to subtract   move this way to add →

Example

Number lines can sometimes have different scales. E.g. they might go up in steps of 5.

What is –3 + 5? Start at –3 and move 5 places in the positive direction:

–4 –3 –2 –1 0 1 2 3   So –3 + 5 = 2

Work out 3 – 6. Start at 3 and move 6 places in the negative direction:

–4 –3 –2 –1 0 1 2 3 4   So 3 – 6 = –3

What temperature is 5 °C colder than –1 °C? Start at –1 and move 5 places in the negative direction:

–6 –5 –4 –3 –2 –1 0 °C   –6 °C

Use These Rules for Combining Signs

+	+	makes	+
+	–	makes	–
–	+	makes	–
–	–	makes	+

These rules are <u>ONLY TO BE USED WHEN</u>:

1) <u>Multiplying</u> or <u>dividing</u>

Example

Find: (invisible + sign)

a) **–3 × 5**   – + makes – so –3 × 5 = **–15**

b) **–18 ÷ –3**   – – makes + so –18 ÷ –3 = **6**

Be careful when squaring or cubing. Squaring a negative number gives a positive number (e.g. –2 × –2 = 4) but cubing a negative number gives a negative number (e.g. –3 × –3 × –3 = –27).

2) <u>Two signs</u> appear <u>next to</u> each other

Example

Work out:

a) **2 + –8**   + – makes – so 2 + –8 = 2 – 8 = **–6**

b) **3 – –9**   – – makes + so 3 – –9 = 3 + 9 = **12**

Negative numbers are so glass half empty...

Combining signs — if they're the same it makes + and if they're different it makes –.

1) Work out: a) –6 + 11   b) –5 – 10   c) –3 × –6   d) 21 ÷ –7

2) On Friday, the temperature in Negaton was –5.6 °C and in Tiverville was –19.7 °C. What was the difference in temperature between Negaton and Tiverville?

Prime Numbers

There's a special type of number you need to know about — the prime numbers...

Prime Numbers Don't Divide by Anything

Prime numbers are all the numbers that only come up in their own times table:

| 2 | 3 | 5 | 7 | 11 | 13 | 17 | 19 | 23 | 29 | 31 | 37... |

The only way to get ANY PRIME NUMBER is: 1 × ITSELF

E.g. The only numbers that multiply to give 3 are 1 × 3
The only numbers that multiply to give 19 are 1 × 19

Example

Show that 18 is not a prime number.

Just find another way to make 18 other than 1 × 18: 3 × 6 = 18

18 divides by other numbers apart from 1 and 18, so it isn't a prime number.

Five Important Facts

1) 1 is NOT a prime number.
2) 2 is the ONLY even prime number.
3) The first four prime numbers are 2, 3, 5 and 7.
4) Prime numbers end in 1, 3, 7 or 9 (2 and 5 are the only exceptions to this rule).
5) But NOT ALL numbers ending in 1, 3, 7 or 9 are primes, as shown here:
(Only the circled ones are primes.)

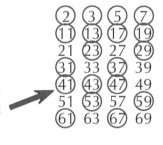

How to Find Prime Numbers — a very simple method

1) All primes (above 5) end in 1, 3, 7 or 9 — ignore any numbers that don't end in one of those.
2) To find which of them ACTUALLY ARE primes, you only need to divide each one by 3 and 7. If it doesn't divide exactly by either 3 or 7 then it's a prime.   *This only works for primes up to 120.*

Example

Find all the prime numbers in this list: 51, 52, 53, 54, 55, 56, 57, 58, 59

1) Get rid of anything that doesn't end in 1, 3, 7 or 9:   51, ~~52~~, 53, ~~54~~, ~~55~~, ~~56~~, 57, ~~58~~, 59

2) Now try dividing 51, 53, 57 and 59 by 3 and 7:

51 ÷ 3 = 17 so 51 is NOT a prime number.
53 ÷ 3 = 17.666... and 53 ÷ 7 = 7.571... so 53 is a prime number.
57 ÷ 3 = 19 so 57 is NOT a prime number.
59 ÷ 3 = 19.666... and 59 ÷ 7 = 8.428... so 59 is a prime number.

So the prime numbers in the list are **53 and 59**.

2 is the only prime that's even — how odd...

1) Write down all the prime numbers from this list: 49, 63, 38, 73, 77, 16, 39, 83

Multiples, Factors and Prime Factors

Ah, welcome to the lovely world of factors — pull up a seat and get ready to learn.

Multiples and Factors

The MULTIPLES of a number are just the values in its <u>times table</u>.

Example

Find the first 5 multiples of 12.

You just need to find the first 5 numbers in the <u>12 times table</u>:   12   24   36   48   60

The FACTORS of a number are all the numbers that <u>divide into it exactly</u>. Here's how to find them:

Example

Find all the factors of 28.

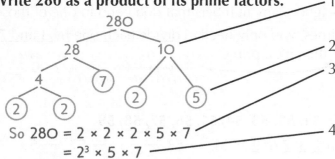

Increasing by 1 each time

$1 \times 28 = 28$
$2 \times 14 = 28$
$\cancel{3 \times}$
$4 \times 7 = 28$
$\cancel{5 \times}$
$\cancel{6 \times}$
$7 \times 4 = 28$

1) Start off with 1 × the number itself, then try 2 ×, then 3 × and so on, <u>listing the pairs</u> in rows.
2) Try each one in turn. <u>Cross out</u> the row if it doesn't divide <u>exactly</u>.
3) Eventually, when you get a number <u>repeated</u>, <u>stop</u>.
4) The factors are the numbers you <u>haven't crossed out</u>.

So the <u>factors of 28</u> are: **1, 2, 4, 7, 14, 28**

Finding Prime Factors — The Factor Tree

<u>Any whole number</u> can be written as a string of prime numbers all multiplied together — this is called a <u>product of prime factors</u>. The easiest way to find it is using a <u>factor tree</u>.

Example

Write 280 as a product of its prime factors.

280
28   10
4   (7)
(2) (2)   (2)   (5)

So 280 = 2 × 2 × 2 × 5 × 7
     = $2^3 \times 5 \times 7$

You could <u>split 280</u> into <u>14 and 20</u> or <u>7 and 40</u> — you'll always get the <u>same</u> product of prime factors.

1) Start with the number at the top, and <u>split</u> it into <u>factors</u> as shown.
2) Every time you get a prime, <u>ring it</u>.
3) Keep going until you can't go further (i.e. you're just left with primes), then write the primes out <u>in order</u>.
4) You might be asked to group numbers that are the same into powers. This is known as using <u>indices</u> (i.e. $2 \times 2 \times 2 = 2^3$).

The prime factors of a number are <u>always the same</u>, no matter how you <u>split it up</u>.
Every number has a <u>unique prime factorisation</u> — no two are the same.

All numbers can be written as a product of prime factors...

1) Find: a) the first 8 multiples of 15   b) all the factors of 64
2) Write down the next two numbers in the number pattern 12, 24, 36, 48, ...
3) a) Write 300 as a product of its prime factors.   b) Write your answer to a) using indices.

Common Multiples and Factors

Next, it's finding numbers that are multiples or factors of two (or more) numbers.

Finding Common Multiples

A common multiple is any number that divides by all the numbers in question.
To find the smallest number that divides by two or more numbers, use one of these two methods:

Method

LIST the MULTIPLES of ALL the numbers. Find the SMALLEST one that's in ALL the lists.

OR

Write out the PRODUCT OF PRIME FACTORS of each number. PAIR UP numbers that appear in BOTH PRODUCTS, and CROSS OUT one of each pair. Then MULTIPLY all the others together.

Example

Find the smallest number that will divide by 3 and 4.

Multiples of 3:   3, 6, 9, (12) 15, ...
Multiples of 4:   4, 8, (12) 16, ...

So the smallest number that divides by 3 and 4 is **12**.

Find the smallest number that will divide by 20 and 28.

20 = (2) × (2) × 5
28 = (2) × (2) × 7

So the smallest number that divides by 20 and 28 is 2 × 2 × 5 × 7 = **140**.

This method's handy when the two numbers are quite big.

You might be asked to find the 'Lowest Common Multiple' (or LCM). This is just a fancy way of saying "the smallest number that will divide by all the numbers in question".

Finding Common Factors

A common factor is any number that will divide into all the numbers in question.
To find the biggest number that divides into two or more numbers, use one of these two methods:

Method

LIST the FACTORS of ALL the numbers. Find the BIGGEST one that's in ALL the lists.

OR

Write out the PRODUCT OF PRIME FACTORS of each number. CIRCLE the numbers that appear in BOTH PRODUCTS, then MULTIPLY these numbers together.

Example

Find the biggest number that will divide into 24, 42 and 84.

Factors of 24 are: 1, 2, 3, 4, (6) 8, 12, 24
Factors of 42 are: 1, 2, 3, (6) 7, 14, 21, 42
Factors of 84 are: 1, 2, 3, 4, (6) 7, 12, 14, 21, 28, 42, 84
So the biggest number that will divide into 24, 42 and 84 is **6**.

Find the biggest number that will divide into 60 and 220.

60 = (2) × (2) × 3 × (5)
220 = (2) × (2) × (5) × 11

So the biggest number that will divide into 60 and 220 is 2 × 2 × 5 = **20**.

Only use the numbers from each pair once.

You might be asked to find the 'Highest Common Factor' (or HCF).
This just means "the biggest number that will divide into the numbers in question".

Make sure you're happy with all of these methods...

1) Find the smallest number that will divide by 9 and 12.   2) Find the HCF of 48, 64 and 80.

Fractions, Decimals and Percentages

Fractions, decimals and percentages are three different ways of describing when you've got part of a whole thing. They're closely related and you can convert between them. This table shows some really common conversions — it'll help you if you know them straight off:

Fractions with a 1 on the top (e.g. $\frac{1}{2}$, $\frac{1}{3}$, $\frac{1}{4}$, etc.) are called unit fractions.

Fraction	Decimal	Percentage
$\frac{1}{2}$	0.5	50%
$\frac{1}{4}$	0.25	25%
$\frac{3}{4}$	0.75	75%
$\frac{1}{8}$	0.125	$12\frac{1}{2}\%$
$\frac{1}{3}$	0.333333...	$33\frac{1}{3}\%$
$\frac{2}{3}$	0.666666...	$66\frac{2}{3}\%$
$\frac{1}{10}$	0.1	10%
$\frac{1}{5}$	0.2	20%
$\frac{2}{5}$	0.4	40%

0.3333... and 0.6666... are known as 'recurring' decimals — the same pattern of numbers carries on repeating itself forever. You might see them written as $0.\dot{3}$ and $0.\dot{6}$.

The more of those conversions you learn, the better — but for those that you <u>don't know</u>, you must <u>also learn</u> how to <u>convert</u> between the three types. These are the methods:

$$\text{Fraction} \xrightarrow{\text{Divide}} \text{Decimal} \xrightarrow{\times \text{ by } 100} \text{Percentage}$$

E.g. $\frac{7}{20}$ is $7 \div 20$ = 0.35   E.g. 0.35×100 = 35%

$$\text{Fraction} \xleftarrow[\text{The awkward one}]{} \text{Decimal} \xleftarrow[\div \text{ by } 100]{} \text{Percentage}$$

<u>Converting decimals to fractions</u> is a bit more awkward.
The digits after the decimal point go on the top, and a <u>power of 10</u> on the bottom — with the same number of zeros as there were decimal places.

$$0.6 = \frac{6}{10} \qquad 0.3 = \frac{3}{10} \qquad 0.7 = \frac{7}{10} \qquad \text{etc.}$$

$$0.12 = \frac{12}{100} \qquad 0.78 = \frac{78}{100} \qquad 0.05 = \frac{5}{100} \qquad \text{etc.}$$

$$0.345 = \frac{345}{1000} \qquad 0.908 = \frac{908}{1000} \qquad 0.024 = \frac{24}{1000} \qquad \text{etc.}$$

These can often be <u>cancelled down</u> — see p.19.

Learn the common conversions — life will be much easier...

1) Turn the following decimals into fractions and reduce them to their simplest form.
   a) 0.8   b) 0.04   c) 0.23   d) 0.999

2) Which is greater: a) 22% or $\frac{3}{9}$?   b) 0.7 or $\frac{17}{25}$?

3) Write these in ascending order: 0.5, 55%, $\frac{1}{5}$

Fractions

This page tells you how to deal with fractions without your calculator.

Equivalent Fractions

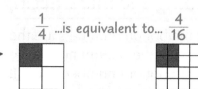

$\frac{1}{4}$ ...is equivalent to... $\frac{4}{16}$

1) <u>Equivalent</u> fractions are <u>equal in size</u>...

2) ...but the <u>numbers</u> on the top and bottom are <u>different</u>.

3) To get from one fraction to an equivalent one —
<u>MULTIPLY top and bottom</u> by the <u>SAME NUMBER</u>.

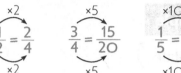

$\times 2$ $\times 5$ $\times 100$

$\frac{1}{2} = \frac{2}{4}$ $\frac{3}{4} = \frac{15}{20}$ $\frac{1}{5} = \frac{100}{500}$

$\times 2$ $\times 5$ $\times 100$

Cancelling Down

1) You sometimes need to <u>simplify</u> a fraction by '<u>cancelling down</u>'.

2) This means <u>DIVIDING top and bottom</u> by the <u>SAME NUMBER</u>.

3) To get the fraction <u>as simple as possible</u>,
you might have to do this <u>more than once</u>.

4) When you <u>can't divide</u> any more the fraction
is said to be in its <u>simplest form</u>, or <u>lowest terms</u>.

$\div 3$

$\frac{3}{15} = \frac{1}{5}$

$\div 3$

$\div 10$ $\div 2$

$\frac{20}{40} = \frac{2}{4} = \frac{1}{2}$

$\div 10$ $\div 2$

Ordering Fractions

E.g. Which is <u>bigger</u>, $\frac{2}{3}$ or $\frac{3}{4}$?

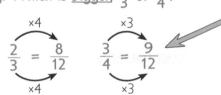

$\times 4$ $\times 3$

$\frac{2}{3} = \frac{8}{12}$ $\frac{3}{4} = \frac{9}{12}$

$\times 4$ $\times 3$

1) Look at the <u>bottom numbers</u> ('denominators')
of the fractions: 3 and 4.

2) Think of a number they will <u>both go into</u> — try <u>12</u>.

3) Change each fraction (make <u>equivalent</u> fractions)
so the <u>bottom number is 12</u>.

4) Now check which is bigger by looking
at their <u>top numbers</u> ('numerators').

5) 9 is <u>bigger</u> than 8, so $\frac{3}{4}$ is bigger than $\frac{2}{3}$.

Mixed Numbers

<u>Mixed numbers</u> have an integer part and a fraction part. Just turn
them into <u>improper fractions</u> first, then you can use them as normal.

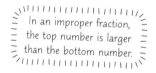

In an improper fraction,
the top number is larger
than the bottom number.

Example

Write $3\frac{4}{5}$ as an improper fraction.

1) Think of the <u>mixed number</u> as an <u>addition</u>:

$3\frac{4}{5} = 3 + \frac{4}{5}$

2) Turn the <u>integer part</u> into a <u>fraction</u>:

$3 + \frac{4}{5} = \frac{15}{5} + \frac{4}{5} = \frac{15+4}{5} = \frac{19}{5}$

Write $\frac{23}{3}$ as a mixed number.

<u>Divide</u> the top number by the bottom.

1) The <u>answer</u> gives the <u>whole number part</u>.

2) The <u>remainder</u> goes <u>on top</u> of the fraction.

$23 \div 3 = 7$ remainder 2   so $\frac{23}{3} = 7\frac{2}{3}$

To simplify, divide top and bottom by the same number...

Have a go at cancelling down and ordering the fractions below — and no cheating with a calculator.

1) Cancel these down as far as possible: a) $\frac{20}{28}$ b) $\frac{9}{36}$

2) Which is bigger, $\frac{5}{8}$ or $\frac{2}{3}$?   3) Write $\frac{43}{7}$ as a mixed number.

Section 1 — Numbers

20

Fractions

Adding and Subtracting

1) If the <u>bottom numbers</u> are the <u>same</u>, add or subtract the <u>TOP NUMBERS ONLY</u>, leaving the bottom number <u>as it is</u>.
2) If the bottom numbers are <u>different</u>, you have to <u>make them the same</u> using <u>equivalent fractions</u> (see page 19).

Example

Calculate $\frac{5}{7} - \frac{3}{7}$

Just <u>subtract</u> the top numbers.
Keep the bottom number the <u>same</u>.

$\frac{5}{7} - \frac{3}{7} = \frac{5-3}{7} = \frac{2}{7}$

Calculate $\frac{1}{4} + \frac{5}{12}$
1) Convert the fractions so they have the <u>same denominator</u>.
$\frac{1}{4} = \frac{3}{12}$
2) Then <u>add</u> as usual.
$\frac{3}{12} + \frac{5}{12} = \frac{3+5}{12} = \frac{8}{12} = \frac{2}{3}$

It's a good idea to try and give your answer in its simplest form.

Multiplying

1) <u>Multiply</u> the <u>top numbers</u> to find the <u>numerator</u>...
2) ...and <u>multiply</u> the <u>bottom numbers</u> to find the <u>denominator</u>.

Example

Calculate $7 \times \frac{2}{5}$
1) Write the whole number as a <u>fraction</u> over 1.
2) Multiply the <u>top</u> and <u>bottom</u> numbers.

$7 \times \frac{2}{5} = \frac{7}{1} \times \frac{2}{5}$
$= \frac{14}{5}$

Example

Calculate $\frac{3}{5} \times \frac{4}{6}$

Multiply the <u>top</u> and <u>bottom</u> numbers.

$\frac{3}{5} \times \frac{4}{6} = \frac{3 \times 4}{5 \times 6} = \frac{12}{30} = \frac{2}{5}$

Additional

Calculate $2\frac{1}{5} \times 4\frac{1}{2}$
1) Write both fractions as <u>improper fractions</u>.
$2\frac{1}{5} = \frac{11}{5}$ and $4\frac{1}{2} = \frac{9}{2}$
2) Then <u>multiply</u> as usual.
$\frac{11}{5} \times \frac{9}{2} = \frac{11 \times 9}{5 \times 2} = \frac{99}{10}$ or $9\frac{9}{10}$

Dividing

1) Turn the 2nd fraction <u>UPSIDE DOWN</u>...
2) ...and then <u>multiply</u>, as shown above.

Numbers turned upside down are called reciprocals. The reciprocal of $\frac{6}{7}$ is $\frac{7}{6}$ and the reciprocal of 3 is $\frac{1}{3}$.

Example

Calculate $4 \div \frac{8}{3}$
1) Find the <u>reciprocal</u> of $\frac{8}{3}$:
$\frac{8}{3} \rightarrow \frac{3}{8}$
2) Then <u>multiply</u> as usual.
$4 \times \frac{3}{8} = \frac{\cancel{4}^1}{1} \times \frac{3}{\cancel{8}_2} = \frac{1}{1} \times \frac{3}{2} = \frac{1 \times 3}{1 \times 2} = \frac{3}{2}$

It always helps to cancel down your fractions before multiplying.

Additional

Calculate $2\frac{4}{5} \div 3\frac{2}{3}$
1) Write both fractions as <u>improper fractions</u>.
$2\frac{4}{5} = \frac{14}{5}$ and $3\frac{2}{3} = \frac{11}{3}$
2) Find the reciprocal of $\frac{11}{3}$ and <u>multiply</u> as usual.
$\frac{14}{5} \times \frac{3}{11} = \frac{14 \times 3}{5 \times 11} = \frac{42}{55}$

Dividing is just like multiplying, but standing on your head...

1) $\frac{3}{10} + \frac{4}{10}$ 2) a) $\frac{2}{3} - \frac{4}{9}$ b) $6 \times \frac{1}{12}$ 3) $\frac{7}{3} \div \frac{2}{9}$ 4) a) $4\frac{3}{5} \times 2\frac{1}{3}$ b) $\frac{59}{8} \div 6\frac{1}{2}$

Section 1 — Numbers

Fractions

This is the final hurdle. The last page exclusively on fractions.
Just make sure you know your stuff by testing yourself on the questions below.

Finding a **Fraction of** Something

1) <u>Multiply</u> the 'something' by the <u>TOP</u> of the fraction...

2) ...then <u>divide</u> it by the <u>BOTTOM</u>.

E.g. $\frac{9}{20}$ of £360 = £360 × 9 ÷ 20
= £162

Depending on the calculation you're doing, it can sometimes be easier to divide by the bottom first, and then multiply by the top.

Example

John eats $\frac{2}{5}$ of a 500 g bar of chocolate. How much chocolate did he eat?

1) <u>Multiply</u> the 'something' by 2: 500 × 2 = 1000

2) Then <u>divide</u> by 5: 1000 ÷ 5 = 200 g

Marcus has 324 songs on his laptop. He deletes 1 out of every four of them. How many songs did he have left?

1) Write 1 out of 4 as a <u>fraction</u>. $\frac{1}{4}$

2) <u>Multiply</u> by 1 and divide by 4. 324 × 1 ÷ 4 = 81

3) <u>Subtract</u> from 324 to find the number of songs <u>left</u>. 324 − 81 = 243

One Thing as a **Fraction of** Another

You can write one <u>number</u> as a fraction of <u>another number</u> just by putting the first number over the second and <u>cancelling down</u>. This works if the first number is <u>bigger</u> than the second number too — you'll just end up with a fraction <u>greater than 1</u>.

E.g. <u>132</u> as a fraction of 144 is $\frac{132}{144} = \frac{11}{12}$, and <u>144</u> as a fraction of 132 is $\frac{144}{132} = \frac{12}{11}$

Example

Claire owns 64 books. 8 of them are fiction. What fraction of her books are fiction?

1) Put the 8 <u>over</u> the 64. $\frac{8}{64}$

2) <u>Simplify</u> your answer. $\frac{8}{64} = \frac{1}{8}$

Write 30 cm as a fraction of 2 m.

1) Convert 2 m into cm so the measurements are in the same units. 2 m = 200 cm

2) Put the 30 <u>over</u> the 200. $\frac{30}{200}$

3) <u>Simplify</u> your answer. $\frac{30}{200} = \frac{3}{20}$

What fraction of this page did you understand?

1) Steph has 32 m of ribbon. She uses $\frac{3}{8}$ of it. How much did she use?

2) $\frac{5}{6}$ of the 354 Z-Factor contestants can't sing. How many contestants can't sing?

3) 12 out of 96 lions at Rugby Zoo like meat. What fraction of the lions dislike meat?

Percentage Basics

These simple percentage questions shouldn't give you much trouble. Especially if you remember:

1) 'Per cent' means 'out of 100', so 20% means '20 out of 100' = $\frac{20}{100}$
2) If a question asks you to work out the percentage OF something you can replace the word OF with a multiplication (×).

Find **x%** of **y**

You can work out simple percentages by turning them into fractions.

The common percentage to fraction conversions are on p.18.

Example

Find 25% of 160.

$25\% = \frac{1}{4}$

25% of 160 = $160 \times \frac{1}{4} = \frac{160}{4} = 40$

Find 60% of 70.

1) $10\% = \frac{1}{10}$, so divide by 10 find 10%: $70 \div 10 = 7$
2) Then multiply 10% by 6 to find 60%: $7 \times 6 = 42$

For trickier percentages, turn the percentage into a decimal, then multiply.

Example

Find 12% of £4.

1) Write 12% as a decimal: $12\% = 12 \div 100 = 0.12$
2) Multiply 0.12 by £4: $0.12 \times £4 = £0.48$

Additional

Find 125% of 600 kg.

1) Write 125% as a decimal: $125\% = 125 \div 100 = 1.25$
2) Multiply 1.25 by 600 kg: $1.25 \times 600\text{ kg} = 750\text{ kg}$

Express **x** as a **Percentage** of **y**

Divide x by y, then multiply by 100.

Example

Give 6p as a percentage of 96p.

Divide 6p by 96p, then multiply by 100:

$(6 \div 96) \times 100 = 6.25\%$

Additional

A pumpkin was originally measured as 90 cm wide. Four weeks later, it was 1.35 m wide. Give its width after four weeks as a percentage of its original width.

1) Write both amounts in the same units — convert 1.35 m to cm.   1.35 m = 135 cm
2) Divide 135 cm by 90 cm, then multiply by 100: $(135 \div 90) \times 100 = 150\%$

Compare Two Quantities Using Percentages

You can compare two quantities by expressing them both as percentages.

Example

Bottle A contains 350 ml of water and has a capacity of 500 ml.
Bottle B contains 400 ml of water and has a capacity of 625 ml. Which bottle is more full?

1) Bottle A: $(350 \div 500) \times 100 = 70\%$
2) Bottle B: $(400 \div 625) \times 100 = 64\%$ 70% is greater than 64% so bottle A is more full.

This stuff is 100% non-stop thrills, guaranteed...

1) Find: a) 39% of 505,   b) 175% of 356.   2) Give 630 m as a percentage of 840 m.

Rounding Numbers and Estimating

You need to be able to use 3 different rounding methods.
We'll do decimal places first, but there's the same basic idea behind all three.

Decimal Places (d.p.)

If you're rounding to 2 d.p. the last digit is the second digit after the decimal point.

To round to a given number of <u>decimal places</u>:

1) <u>Identify</u> the position of the '<u>last digit</u>' from the number of decimal places.
2) Then look at the next digit to the <u>right</u> — called <u>the decider</u>.
3) If the <u>decider</u> is <u>5 or more</u>, then <u>round up</u> the <u>last digit</u>.
   If the <u>decider</u> is <u>4 or less</u>, then leave the <u>last digit</u> as it is.
4) There must be <u>no more digits</u> after the last digit (not even zeros).

Example

What is 21.84 correct to <u>1 decimal place</u>?

$$21.\underline{8}\underline{4} = 21.8$$

<u>LAST DIGIT</u> to be written (1st decimal place because we're rounding to 1 d.p.)

DECIDER

The <u>LAST DIGIT</u> stays the <u>same</u> because the <u>DECIDER</u> is <u>4 or less</u>.

Example

What is 39.7392739 to <u>2 decimal places</u>?

$$39.7\underline{3}\underline{9}2739 = 39.74$$

<u>LAST DIGIT</u> to be written (2nd decimal place because we're rounding to 2 d.p.)

DECIDER

The <u>LAST DIGIT</u> rounds <u>UP</u> because the <u>DECIDER</u> is <u>5 or more</u>.

Watch Out for **Pesky Nines**

If you have to <u>round up</u> a <u>9</u> (to 10), replace the 9 with 0, and <u>add 1</u> to the digit on the <u>left</u>.

Example

a) **Round 48.897 to 2 d.p.**

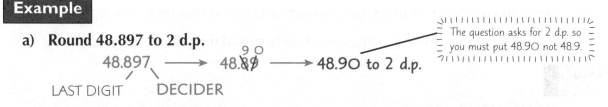

$$48.897 \longrightarrow 48.89 \longrightarrow 48.90 \text{ to 2 d.p.}$$

LAST DIGIT   DECIDER

The question asks for 2 d.p. so you must put 48.90 not 48.9.

b) **Use a calculator to work out 638 ÷ (2 × 32). Round your answer to 1 d.p.**

$$638 ÷ (2 × 32) = 9.96875 \longrightarrow 9.96 \longrightarrow 10.0 \text{ to 1 d.p.}$$

Be extra careful when the last digit is a 9...

1) Give: a) 23.568 correct to 1 d.p.   b) 6.789 correct to 2 d.p.
2) Use a calculator to work out: a) 79 × (41 ÷ 24) to 1 d.p.   b) 377 ÷ (7 × 11) to 2 d.p.

Rounding Numbers and Estimating

To the **Nearest Whole Number, Ten, Hundred** etc.

You can round to the <u>nearest whole number</u>, <u>ten</u>, <u>tenth</u>, <u>hundred</u>, <u>thousandth</u> and so on.

1) <u>Identify the last digit</u>, e.g. for the nearest <u>whole number</u> it's the <u>ones</u> position.
2) <u>Round the last digit</u> and <u>fill in with zeros</u> up to the decimal point.

Example

Round 61 729 to the nearest <u>thousand</u>.

<u>LAST DIGIT</u> is in the 'thousands' position.   Fill in <u>3 zeros</u> up to decimal point.

$$61729 = 62000$$

<u>DECIDER</u> is 5 or more. ⟶ Last digit <u>rounds up</u>.

Significant Figures (s.f.)

The <u>1st significant figure</u> of any number is <u>the first digit which isn't a zero</u>.

The <u>2nd, 3rd, etc. significant figures</u> follow straight after the 1st — they're allowed to be zeros.

To <u>round</u> to a given number of significant figures:

1) Find the <u>last digit</u> — e.g. for 3 s.f., it's the 3rd <u>significant figure</u>.
2) Use the digit to the right of it as the <u>decider</u>, just like for d.p.
3) Once you've rounded, <u>fill up</u> with <u>zeros</u>, up to but <u>not beyond</u> the decimal point.

0.00230
S.F: 1st 2nd 3rd

Example

Round 1276.7 to <u>3 significant figures</u>.

<u>LAST DIGIT</u> is the 3rd sig. fig.   Need a <u>zero</u> to fill up to decimal point.

$$1276.7 = 1280$$

<u>DECIDER</u> is 5 or more. ⟶ Last digit <u>rounds up</u>.

There's only one significant figure around here...

Estimating

Estimating can help you to work out a <u>rough answer</u> or <u>check</u> your answer is roughly correct.

<u>Round everything off</u> to <u>nice convenient numbers</u> and then work out the answer.

Example

Estimate $\frac{65.26 \times 116.2}{1.89}$.

<u>Round</u> each number to something easy, then do the calculation with the rounded numbers.

≈ means 'approximately equal to'

$$\frac{65.26 \times 116.2}{1.89} \approx \frac{65 \times 100}{2} = \frac{6500}{2} = 3250$$

All this rounding is making me dizzy...

1) Round: a) 17.548 to the nearest whole number   b) 51 655 to the nearest hundred
2) Round 0.256 to 2 significant figures.   3) Estimate 17.3 × 31.87.

Powers and Roots

They may look small, but they're quite mighty. Take a look at these powers and roots.

Powers are Useful Shorthand

$2^3 = 2 \times 2 \times 2$

$2^5 = 2 \times 2 \times 2 \times 2 \times 2$

1) Powers tell you how many of the same number are multiplied together, e.g. $3^4 = 3 \times 3 \times 3 \times 3$.

2) Find powers using your calculator by pressing the $x^\blacksquare$ key. E.g. 9 $x^\blacksquare$ 4 $=$ gives $9^4 = 6561$.

3) Anything to the power 1 is itself, e.g. $4^1 = 4$.

4) Anything to the power 0 is 1, e.g. $12^0 = 1$.

5) Negative numbers raised to a power can be positive or negative, depending on whether the power is even or odd, e.g. $(-3)^2 = -3 \times -3 = 9$, but $(-3)^3 = -3 \times -3 \times -3 = -27$.

$2^2 = 4$	$2^3 = 8$	$2^4 = 16$	$2^5 = 32$
$3^2 = 9$	$3^3 = 27$	$3^4 = 81$	$3^5 = 243$
$4^2 = 16$	$4^3 = 64$	$4^4 = 256$	$4^5 = 1024$
$5^2 = 25$	$5^3 = 125$	$5^4 = 625$	$5^5 = 3125$

Square Roots

'Squared' means 'multiplied by itself': $6^2 = 6 \times 6 = 36$
SQUARE ROOT $\sqrt{\ }$ is the reverse process: $\sqrt{36} = 6$

'Square Root' means 'What number **times by itself** gives...'

Example

What is $\sqrt{81}$?
9 times itself gives 81. $81 = 9 \times 9$ So $\sqrt{81} = 9$

What is $\sqrt{7.84}$?
Press: $\sqrt{\ }$ 7.84 $=$ 2.8

Find both square roots of 100.
$10 \times 10 = 100$
$-10 \times -10 = 100$
so $\sqrt{100} = 10$ and -10

All numbers also have a negative square root — it's just the '–' version of the normal positive one.

Cube Roots

'Cubed' means 'multiplied by itself and then by itself again': $2^3 = 2 \times 2 \times 2 = 8$
CUBE ROOT $\sqrt[3]{\ }$ is the reverse process: $\sqrt[3]{8} = 2$

'Cube Root' means 'What number **times by itself** and then by **itself again** gives...'

Example

What is $\sqrt[3]{27}$?
3 times itself and then by itself again gives 27. $27 = 3 \times 3 \times 3$ So $\sqrt[3]{27} = 3$

Unlike square roots, there is only one answer.

What is $\sqrt[3]{4913}$?
Press: $\sqrt[3]{\ }$ 4913 $=$ 17

Roots aren't always Exact

Sometimes a number can only be given exactly using a $\sqrt{\ }$ sign.
For example, $\sqrt{2} = 1.41421...$ can be rounded to 1.4 but $1.4^2 = 1.96$, not 2.
So, if you're asked for an exact answer you'll need to write $\sqrt{2}$.

Don't forget about the negative square root...

1) Write down all the square and cube numbers between 3 and 99.

2) Calculate: a) $9^2 + 1^4$ b) the square root of 121   c) the cube root of 512

Standard Form

Standard form (or 'standard index form') is useful for writing very big or very small numbers in a more convenient way. A number written in standard form must always be in exactly this form:

This <u>number</u> must <u>always</u> be <u>between 1 and 10</u>.
(The fancy way of saying this is $1 \leq A < 10$)

$$A \times 10^n$$

This number is just the <u>number of places</u> the <u>decimal point</u> moves.

Three Rules for Standard Form

1) The <u>front number</u> must always be between <u>1 and 10</u>.
2) The power of 10, n, is <u>how far the decimal point moves</u>.
3) n is <u>positive</u> for <u>big</u> numbers, n is <u>negative</u> for <u>small</u> numbers.

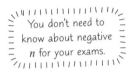
You don't need to know about negative n for your exams.

Three Important Examples

Example

Express 259 000 in standard form.

1) <u>Move the decimal point</u> until 259 000 becomes 2.59 ($1 \leq A < 10$).
2) The decimal point has moved <u>5 places</u> so $n = 5$, giving 10^5.

2.59000

$= 2.59 \times 10^5$

Example

Write these numbers in order from smallest to largest:
2.25×10^4 7.98×10^2 6880 3.12×10^4 6.75×10^3 134 000

1) First <u>convert</u> all the numbers into standard form.
   $6880 = 6.88 \times 10^3$ $134\,000 = 1.34 \times 10^5$

2) Now <u>group</u> the numbers with the <u>same power</u> together and order them based on the power.
   7.98×10^2 6.88×10^3 6.75×10^3 2.25×10^4 3.12×10^4 1.34×10^5

3) Finally <u>order each group</u> by the <u>size</u> of the <u>front number</u>
   — give the numbers in the form they are given in the question.
   7.98×10^2 6.75×10^3 6880 2.25×10^4 3.12×10^4 134 000

Example

Use a calculator to work out $8.5 \times 10^4 \times 2.43 \times 10^2$.
Give your answer in standard form correct to 3 s.f.

1) Work out the calculation.
2) <u>Round</u> your answer to 3 s.f.
3) Then <u>convert</u> the answer into standard form.

$8.5 \times 10^4 \times 2.43 \times 10^2 = 20\,655\,000$
20 655 000 rounds to 20 700 000
$20\,700\,000 = 2.07 \times 10^7$

Always always always make sure 'A' is between 1 and 10...

1) Express these numbers in standard form: a) 19 000 000   b) 65 700

Warm-Up and Practice Questions

Have a go at the warm-up questions below to make sure you've properly taken this section in.
Then when you're ready, go on to the practice questions and get your maths muscles flexing.

Warm-Up Questions

Don't use a calculator for any of these Warm-Up questions.

1) Work out: a) $3 + 2 \times 6$ b) $24 \div (6 - 2)$ c) $\dfrac{5 \times 3 + 1}{6 + 4 \div 2}$

2) Put the following in order from smallest to biggest:
   0.23   −0.76   2.03   −1.4   1.23

3) Work out: a) $23.6 + 19.8$ b) $274 - 136$ c) $145 + 37 - 112$

4) Work out: a) 16×27 b) $228 \div 12$ c) 5.4×8.3

5) Find the lowest common multiple of 6 and 8.

6) Find, in their simplest form: a) $\frac{2}{3} + \frac{1}{6}$ b) $\frac{7}{12} - \frac{5}{9}$ c) $\frac{3}{8} \times \frac{2}{5}$ d) $\frac{7}{16} \div \frac{3}{4}$

7) Find: a) 20% of 120   b) 75% of £800   c) 125% of 360

8) Round 4173 to the: a) nearest ten   b) nearest hundred   c) nearest thousand

9) Work out: a) $\sqrt{25}$ b) $\sqrt{144}$ c) $\sqrt[3]{64}$

10) a) Write 4.52×10^4 as an ordinary number.
    b) Write 708 000 in standard form.

Practice Questions

1) a) Find all the factors of the following numbers.

   22   1, 2, 11, 22 ....

   41   1, 41 ....

   33   1, 3, 11, 33 ....

   110   1, 2, 5, 10, 11, 22, 55, 110 ....
                                                                          [4 marks]

   b) Which of the four numbers above is prime? Give a reason for your answer.

   41 is the only prime number. It is the only number from the list ....

   where the factors are just 1 and itself. ....
                                                                          [2 marks]

   c) What is the biggest number that will divide into 22, 33 and 110?

   *Look at the lists above to find the biggest
   number that is a factor of 22, 33 and 110.*

                                        ....11..........
                                                                          [1 mark]

Practice Questions

2) Place the following numbers in order, beginning with the smallest.

$$0.12 \qquad 17\% \qquad \frac{1}{20} \qquad \frac{13}{100} \qquad 9\% \qquad \frac{9}{50}$$

....

[3 marks]

3) Use BODMAS to work out the values of the following calculations.

a) $5 - 6 \times 4 + 5$

....

[2 marks]

b) $\dfrac{55 \times 10 \div 5}{4 \times 5 - 9}$

....

[2 marks]

4) Calculate:

a) 17.8×5

Don't use a calculator for this question.

....

[2 marks]

b) $9.44 - 5.7$

....

[2 marks]

5) Write 84 as a product of its prime factors.

....

[2 marks]

Practice Questions

6) a) Which of the following is the best estimate of the answer to $61.24 \div 5.92$?

      6   7   8   9   10   11

....

[1 mark]

b) Which of the following is the best estimate of the answer to 121.6×0.49?

      6   6.5   60   65   600   650

....

[1 mark]

c) Estimate the answer to $\dfrac{38.4 \times 28.2}{6.17 \times 2.02}$.

....

[2 marks]

7) Find:

Don't use a calculator for this question.

a) 15% of 40

....

[2 marks]

b) $\dfrac{7}{9}$ of 45

....

[2 marks]

8) A car originally cost £12 000. It is sold for £4800.
Find the sale price of the car as a percentage of its original cost.

....

[2 marks]

Practice Questions

9) Evaluate the following to two decimal places.

   a) $\sqrt{142}$

....
[1 mark]

   b) $\sqrt[3]{82}$

....
[1 mark]

   c) $\sqrt[5]{1986}$

....
[1 mark]

10) a)   In a bag of 21 marbles, $\frac{2}{7}$ of them are blue, $\frac{1}{3}$ are red and the rest are green. How many green marbles are in the bag?

Don't use a calculator for this question.

....
[3 marks]

   b)   A sack of bird seed weighs 15 kg. How many $\frac{3}{4}$ kg bags can be filled from one sack?

....
[3 marks]

11) In an online shop, 3×10^4 purchases were made in one day.
The total amount spent on the day was £1.5 million.

Calculate the average amount spent on each purchase.

....
[3 marks]

Summary Questions

Well, that's Section 1 done — have a go at these questions to see how much you can remember.
- Try these questions and <u>tick off each one</u> when you <u>get it right</u>.
- When you've done <u>all the questions</u> for a topic and are <u>completely happy</u>, tick off the topic.

Only use your calculator when the question tells you to.

Ordering Numbers and Calculations (p.3-13) ☐

1) Find the value of: a) $4 + 10 \div 2$ b) $12 \div 3 \times 2$ c) $(8 + 12) \div 20$
2) Work out the following by dividing by factors: a) $270 \div 18$ b) $210 \div 35$
3) Put these numbers in ascending order: 0.02, 54, –11.8, 23.91, –0.09, 0.001, –0.51, 0.9
4) On Day 1 it was –6 °C, Day 2 was –8 °C and Day 3 was –7.5 °C. Which day was coldest?
5) Work out: a) $417 + 194$ b) $753 - 157$ c) $(2.3 + 1.123) - 0.75$
6) Find: a) 1.223×100 b) 15.12×1000 c) $6.75 \div 10$ d) $1.24 \div 200$
7) Work out: a) 131×19 b) $672 \div 14$ c) 9.12×34 d) $65.65 \div 13$

Types of Number, Factors and Multiples (p.14-17) ☐

8) Work out: a) $-8 + 6$ b) $-4 - 10$ c) -7×-8 d) $81 \div -9$
9) Find all the prime numbers between: a) 40 and 50   b) 80 and 90
10) Find: a) the first 5 multiples of 13   b) all the factors of 36
11) Express 252 as the product of prime factors.
12) Find the highest number that divides into both 28 and 40.

Fractions, Decimals and Percentages (p.18-22) ☐

13) Write: a) 0.6 as a fraction and a percentage   b) 65% as a fraction and a decimal
14) Give two fractions equivalent to $\frac{3}{5}$.
15) Work out: a) $\frac{2}{8} + \frac{3}{8}$ b) $\frac{4}{5} - \frac{2}{5}$ c) $\frac{1}{9} + \frac{4}{9}$
16) Simplify: a) $\frac{1}{3} + \frac{5}{9}$ b) $\frac{7}{10} - \frac{1}{2}$ c) $\frac{7}{10} \times \frac{5}{6}$ d) $\frac{2}{11} \div \frac{3}{10}$
17) Simplify: a) $\frac{4}{9} + 1\frac{1}{3}$ b) $2\frac{1}{4} - \frac{5}{8}$ c) $4\frac{1}{2} \times 2\frac{1}{4}$ d) $3\frac{2}{3} \div -\frac{1}{6}$
18) Calculate: a) $\frac{2}{9}$ of 540   b) $\frac{3}{7}$ of 490   c) 15% of 78   d) 180% of £95
19) Use a calculator to give: a) 7 as a fraction of 182   b) 61p as a percentage of £15.25

Rounding and Estimating (p.23-24) ☐

20) Round: a) 164.353 to 1 d.p.   b) 765 444 to the nearest ten
21) Round: a) 76 233 to 2 s.f.   b) 25.65 to 1 s.f.
22) Estimate the value of: a) 22.2×50.3 b) $\frac{20.5 \times 4.9}{9.7}$ c) $\frac{498 \times 98}{53}$

Powers, Roots and Standard Form (p.25-26) ☐

23) Which of these numbers are square numbers?   16   38   44   49   121   125
24) Use a calculator to find: a) $\sqrt{249.64}$ b) $\sqrt[3]{2744}$
25) Express: a) 2×10^8 as an ordinary number   b) 4 300 000 in standard form
26) Which of these numbers is the biggest? 5.4×10^6 452 000 4.55×10^5 56 000 000

Section 2 — Algebra

Algebra — Simplifying Terms

Make sure you understand and learn these basic rules for dealing with algebraic expressions.

Terms

Before you can do anything else with algebra, you must understand what a <u>term</u> is:

> A TERM IS EITHER A NUMBER, A LETTER OR COLLECTION
> OF NUMBERS OR LETTERS MULTIPLIED/DIVIDED TOGETHER

Terms are separated by <u>+ and – signs</u>. Every term has a + or – attached to the <u>front of it</u>.

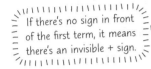 If there's no sign in front of the first term, it means there's an invisible + sign.

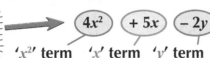 $4x^2$ $+5x$ $-2y$ $+6y^2$ $+4$

'x^2' term   'x' term   'y' term   'y^2' term   'number' term

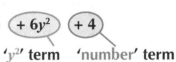 $6y^2$ means $6 \times y^2$ — see page 29.

Simplifying or 'Collecting Like Terms'

To <u>simplify</u> an algebraic expression made up of all the <u>same terms</u>, just <u>add</u> or <u>subtract</u> them.

Example

'r' just means '$1r$'.

Simplify $r + r + r + r$.
Just <u>add up</u> all the r's:

$r + r + r + r = \mathbf{4r}$

Simplify $2s + 3s - s$.
Again, just <u>combine the terms</u> — don't forget there's a '–' before the last s:

$2s + 3s - s = \mathbf{4s}$

To <u>simplify</u> an algebraic expression with a mixture of <u>different letters</u> and <u>numbers</u>, you combine '<u>like terms</u>' (e.g. all the x terms, all the y terms, all the number terms, etc.).

Example

Simplify $7x + 3 - x - 2$.

1) Put <u>bubbles</u> round each term — be sure you capture the $+$ or $-$ <u>sign</u> in front of each.
2) Then you can move the bubbles into the <u>best order</u> so that <u>like terms</u> are together.
3) <u>Combine like terms</u>.

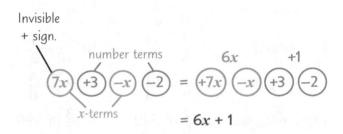

Invisible + sign.   number terms $6x$ $+1$

$(7x)(+3)(-x)(-2)$ = $(+7x)(-x)(+3)(-2)$

x-terms

$= \mathbf{6x + 1}$

Negative Numbers

The negative number rules from page 14 also apply to algebra — so make sure you learn them.

+ +	makes	+
+ –	makes	–
– +	makes	–
– –	makes	+

Use these rules when:
1) <u>Multiplying or dividing</u>. E.g. $-2 \times 3 = -6$, $-4p \div -2 = +2p$
2) <u>Two signs are together</u>. E.g. $5 - -4 = 5 + 4 = 9$, $-x + -y = -x - y$

If only everything in maths could be simplified...

1) Simplify a) $a + a + a$ b) $3d + 7d - 2d$ c) $8x - y - 2x + 3y$
2) Simplify a) $-3 \times 4f$ b) $-5x \times -5$ c) $3a - -b$

Algebra — Simplifying Terms

On this page we'll look at some rules that will help you simplify expressions that have letters and numbers multiplied together.

Letters **Multiplied** Together

Watch out for these combinations of letters in algebra that regularly catch people out:

1) abc means $a \times b \times c$ and $3a$ means $3 \times a$. The ×'s are often left out to make it clearer.

2) gn^2 means $g \times n \times n$. Note that only the n is squared, not the g as well.

3) $(gn)^2$ means $g \times g \times n \times n$. The brackets mean that <u>BOTH</u> letters are squared.

4) <u>Powers</u> tell you <u>how many</u> letters are multiplied together — so $r^6 = r \times r \times r \times r \times r \times r$.

Example

Careful — h multiplied by itself then by itself again is h^3, not $3h$ ($3h$ means $h + h + h$ or $3 \times h$).

Simplify $h \times h \times h$.

You have 3 h's <u>multiplied together</u>:

$h \times h \times h = h^3$

Simplify $3r \times 2s \times 2$.

Multiply the <u>numbers</u> together, then the <u>letters</u> together:

$3r \times 2s \times 2 = 3 \times 2 \times 2 \times r \times s = \textbf{12}\textbf{\textit{rs}}$

Power Rules in Algebra

You can use these <u>power rules</u> on <u>algebraic expressions</u>:

1) When <u>multiplying</u>, you <u>add</u> the powers.

2) When <u>dividing</u>, you <u>subtract</u> the powers.

3) When doing a <u>power to a power</u>, you <u>multiply</u> the powers.

Example

Simplify $n^5 \times n^2$.
You're multiplying, so <u>add</u> the powers:
$n^5 \times n^2 = n^{5+2} = \textbf{\textit{n}}^\textbf{7}$

Simplify $m^{13} \div m^5$.
You're dividing, so <u>subtract</u> the powers:
$m^{13} \div m^5 = m^{13-5} = \textbf{\textit{m}}^\textbf{8}$

Simplify $(s^2)^5$.
You're doing power to a power, so <u>multiply</u> the powers:
$(s^2)^5 = s^{2\times5} = \textbf{\textit{s}}^\textbf{10}$

Algebraic Fractions

If you have a <u>fraction</u> with letters and numbers, then you might be able to <u>simplify</u>. Just do it the same way you would with a normal fraction.

Example

In equations, the number written before a letter is called the coefficient. You should write it as a whole number or a fraction.

Simplify $\frac{5r}{20}$.
Divide the top and bottom by 5:

$\frac{5r}{20} = \frac{r}{4}$

Simplify $\frac{7e}{e}$.
Divide the top and bottom by e:

$\frac{7e}{e} = \frac{7}{1} = 7$

Power rules make simplifying terms a doddle...

1) Simplify: a) $d \times d \times d \times d \times d$ b) $2e \times 8f$ c) $p^6 \times p^4$ d) $\frac{8j}{2}$

2) Simplify: a) $\frac{4m}{m}$ b) $\frac{20f}{2f}$ c) $\frac{15c^3}{5c}$ d) $\frac{(2ef^3)^2}{f^2}$

Algebra — Multiplying Out Brackets

Multiplying out brackets (also called 'expanding brackets') can be a bit tough.
No need to panic though — here's how it's done.

Multiplying by a **Number**

1) The number <u>outside</u> the brackets multiplies <u>each separate term</u> inside the brackets.

2) A minus <u>outside</u> the brackets <u>reverses</u> all the signs <u>inside</u> the brackets when you multiply.

Example

Expand $3(x + 1)$.

Just <u>multiply</u> 3 by x, then 3 by 1:

$3(x + 1) = (3 \times x) + (3 \times 1)$
$\qquad\qquad = 3x + 3$

Expand $-2(4y - 5)$.

<u>Multiply</u> -2 by $4y$
then -2 by -5:

Two negatives make a positive (see p.32).

$-2(4y - 5)$
$= (-2 \times 4y) + (-2 \times -5)$
$= -8y + 10$

Multiplying by a **Letter**

This is basically the same as multiplying by a <u>number</u>. Remember, when <u>letters</u> are multiplied together, they are just written <u>next to</u> each other, e.g. $p \times q = pq$ (page 33).

Example

Expand $a(b + 2)$.

<u>Multiply</u> a by b, then a by 2.

$a(b + 2) = (a \times b) + (a \times 2)$
$\qquad\qquad = ab + 2a$

Expand $3cd(5e - 2f)$.

<u>Multiply</u> $3cd$ by $5e$, then $3cd$ by $-2f$.

$3cd(5e - 2f) = (3cd \times 5e) + (3cd \times -2f)$
$\qquad\qquad\qquad = 15cde - 6cdf$

Multiplying to get **Powers**

1) If the letter outside the bracket is the same as a letter inside, then you'll end up with a <u>power</u>.

2) Remember, $a \times a = a^2$, and xy^2 means $x \times y \times y$, but $(xy)^2$ means $x \times x \times y \times y$ (see p.33).

Example

Expand $y(y + 5)$.

Multiply y by y, then y by 5.

$y(y + 5) = (y \times y) + (y \times 5)$
$\qquad\qquad = y^2 + 5y$

Expand $-r^2(2r - 7s)$.

<u>Multiply</u> $-r^2$ by $2r$,
then $-r^2$ by $-7s$.

$r^2 \times s = r^2s$

$-r^2(2r - 7s)$
$= (-r^2 \times 2r) + (-r^2 \times -7s)$
$= -2r^3 + 7r^2s$

Remember to collect like terms after you've expanded...

1) Expand: a) $2(4 - x)$ b) $6(2x - 3y)$

2) Expand and simplify $5 - 2(x + 2)$.

3) Expand: a) $h(8 - d)$ b) $2j(3 - j)$ c) $3b^2(a - 2b)$

Algebra — Factorising and Proof

Now it's time to put the brackets back in — this is called factorising. Just follow these three rules:

> 1) Take out the <u>biggest common factor</u> that goes into all the terms.
> 2) Open the brackets and fill in all the bits needed to <u>reproduce each term</u>.
> 3) <u>Check</u> your answer by <u>multiplying out</u> the brackets again.

Taking Out a **Number**

This is the <u>exact reverse</u> of multiplying out brackets. Look for a <u>common factor</u> of the numbers in both terms and take it <u>outside</u> the brackets. The biggest common factor is the <u>biggest number</u> that the numbers in <u>both terms</u> divide by.

Example

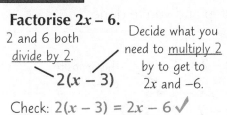

Factorise $2x - 6$.
2 and 6 both <u>divide by 2</u>.
Decide what you need to <u>multiply 2</u> by to get to $2x$ and -6.
$2(x - 3)$
Check: $2(x - 3) = 2x - 6$ ✓

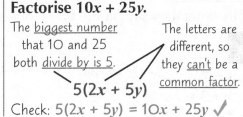

Factorise $10x + 25y$.
The <u>biggest number</u> that 10 and 25 both <u>divide by is 5</u>.
The letters are different, so they <u>can't</u> be a <u>common factor</u>.
$5(2x + 5y)$
Check: $5(2x + 5y) = 10x + 25y$ ✓

Simplify $\dfrac{5x + 5y}{5}$.
$\dfrac{5x + 5y}{5} = \dfrac{5(x + y)}{5} = x + y$
Take out a <u>factor</u> of 5 on the top, then <u>cancel</u> the 5's on the top and bottom.

Taking Out a **Letter**

If the <u>same letter</u> appears in <u>all</u> the terms (but to <u>different powers</u>), you can take out some <u>power</u> of the <u>letter</u> as a <u>common factor</u>. You might be able to take out a <u>number</u> as well.

Example

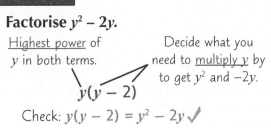

Factorise $y^2 - 2y$.
<u>Highest power</u> of y in both terms.
Decide what you need to <u>multiply y</u> by to get y^2 and $-2y$.
$y(y - 2)$
Check: $y(y - 2) = y^2 - 2y$ ✓

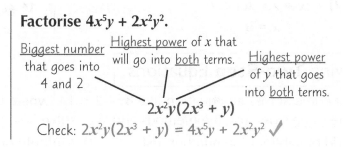

Factorise $4x^5y + 2x^2y^2$.
<u>Biggest number</u> that goes into 4 and 2
<u>Highest power</u> of x that will go into <u>both</u> terms.
<u>Highest power</u> of y that goes into <u>both</u> terms.
$2x^2y(2x^3 + y)$
Check: $2x^2y(2x^3 + y) = 4x^5y + 2x^2y^2$ ✓

Algebraic **Proof**

You can use what you've learned on the last few pages to <u>prove</u> algebraic statements. Usually, you'll have to do a bit of <u>rearranging</u> to show that something is <u>true</u>.

Example

Show that $4(3x - 4) - 8(x - 3)$ can be written as $4(x + 2)$.

1) <u>Multiply out</u> each set of brackets.

$4(3x - 4) - 8(x - 3)$
$= 12x - 16 - 8x + 24$

2) <u>Simplify</u> the expression by <u>collecting like terms</u>. $= 4x + 8$
3) Then <u>factorise</u> to show the correct result. $= 4(x + 2)$ ■

Either write 'QED' or draw a square like this at the end of your proof to show that it's finished.

Common factor? Aww, I was hoping for a rare one...

1) Factorise fully: a) $4 - 10r$ b) $6x + 2y$ c) $30s + 12$ d) $-40 - 24t$
2) Factorise fully: a) $a^2 + 4a$ b) $9b^2 - 3b$ c) $9c^2d + 12cd^3$

Solving Equations

To solve equations, you must find the value of x (or any given letter) that makes the equation true.
To find this value of x, rearrange the equation until you end up with '$x =$' on one side.
Here are a few important points to remember when rearranging.

Golden Rules

1) Always do the SAME thing to both sides of the equation.
2) To get rid of something, do the opposite.
   The opposite of + is − and the opposite of − is +.
   The opposite of × is ÷ and the opposite of ÷ is ×.
3) Keep going until you have a letter on its own.

Solving One-Step Equations

One-step equations are exactly what they say on the tin — one step and you're done.

Example

Solve $x + 3 = 7$.

This means 'take away 3 from both sides'.

The opposite of +3 is −3.

$x + 3 = 7$
$(-3) \quad x + 3 - 3 = 7 - 3$
$x = 4$

Solve $x - 2 = 3$.

The opposite of −2 is +2.

$x - 2 = 3$
$(+2) \quad x - 2 + 2 = 3 + 2$
$x = 5$

Example

Solve $2x = 10$.

$2x$ means $2 \times x$, so do the opposite — divide both sides by 2.

$2x = 10$
$(\div 2) \quad 2x \div 2 = 10 \div 2$
$x = 5$

Solve $\frac{x}{2} = 4$.

$\frac{x}{2}$ means $x \div 2$, so do the opposite — multiply both sides by 2.

$\frac{x}{2} = 4$
$(\times 2) \quad \frac{x}{2} \times 2 = 4 \times 2$
$x = 8$

Solving Two-Step Equations

If you come across an equation like $8x - 2 = 14$ (where there's an x-term and a number on the same side), use the methods above to solve it — just do it in two steps:

1) Add or subtract the number first. 2) Multiply or divide to get '$x =$'.

Example

Solve $5x + 2 = 12$.

$5x + 2 = 12$ — The opposite of +2 is −2.
$(-2) \quad 5x + 2 - 2 = 12 - 2$
$5x = 10$ — The opposite of ×5 is ÷5.
$(\div 5) \quad 5x \div 5 = 10 \div 5$
$x = 2$

Solve $-8 = 3x - 6$.

$-8 = 3x - 6$ — The opposite of −6 is +6.
$(+6) \quad -8 + 6 = 3x - 6 + 6$
$-2 = 3x$ — The opposite of ×3 is ÷3.
$(\div 3) \quad -2 \div 3 = 3x \div 3$
$-\frac{2}{3} = x$, so $x = -\frac{2}{3}$

Always do the same thing to both sides of the equation...

It's a good idea to write down what you're doing at every stage in brackets. Try it out:

1) Solve these equations: a) $x + 6 = 9$ b) $x - 2 = 9$ c) $9x = 27$ d) $\frac{x}{3} = 7$
2) Solve these equations: a) $8 = 4x + 5$ b) $-2 = 3x - 7$
3) Solve these equations: a) $\frac{x}{2} - 3 = 7$ b) $2 - 7x = -5$

Solving Equations

You're not done with solving equations yet — not by a long shot. This is where it gets really fun.

Equations with an 'x' on Both Sides

For equations like $3x + 1 = x - 7$ (where there's an x-term on <u>each side</u>), you have to:

1) Get all the x's on one side and all the <u>numbers</u> on the other.
2) <u>Multiply or divide</u> to get '$x =$ '.

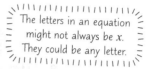

The letters in an equation might not always be x. They could be any letter.

Example

Solve the equation $5x - 7 = 3x + 3$.

$$5x - 7 = 3x + 3$$
$(- 3x)\quad 5x - 7 - 3x = 3x + 3 - 3x$ — To get the x's on only one side, <u>subtract $3x$</u> from each side.
$$2x - 7 = 3$$
$(+ 7)\quad 2x - 7 + 7 = 3 + 7$ — Now <u>add 7</u> to get the numbers on the other side.
$$2x = 10$$
$(\div 2)\quad 2x \div 2 = 10 \div 2$ — The opposite of ×2 is ÷2, so <u>divide both sides by 2</u>.
$$x = 5$$

Equations with Brackets

If the equation has <u>brackets</u> in, you have to <u>multiply out</u> the brackets before solving it as above.

Example

Solve $3(3x - 2) = 5x + 10$.

$$3(3x - 2) = 5x + 10$$ — Multiply out the brackets.
$$9x - 6 = 5x + 10$$
$(- 5x)\quad 9x - 6 - 5x = 5x + 10 - 5x$ — To get the x's on only one side, <u>subtract $5x$</u> from each side.
$$4x - 6 = 10$$
$(+ 6)\quad 4x - 6 + 6 = 10 + 6$ — The opposite of −6 is +6, so <u>add 6</u> to each side.
$$4x = 16$$
$(\div 4)\quad 4x \div 4 = 16 \div 4$ — The opposite of ×4 is ÷4, so <u>divide both sides by 4</u>.
$$x = 4$$

Example

Solve the equation $3(x - 1) = 2(x + 2)$.

$$3(x - 1) = 2(x + 2)$$ — Multiply out the brackets.
$$3x - 3 = 2x + 4$$
$(- 2x)\quad 3x - 3 - 2x = 2x + 4 - 2x$ — To get the x's on only one side, <u>subtract $2x$</u> from each side.
$$x - 3 = 4$$
$(+ 3)\quad x - 3 + 3 = 4 + 3$ — The opposite of −3 is +3, so <u>add 3</u> to each side.
$$x = 7$$

Finding x? It's always in the last place you think to look...

1) Solve $3x - 5 = 4x + 5$.   2) Solve $4(3x - 1) = 2$.   3) Solve $2(2x - 3) = 6(x - 2)$.

Solving Equations

Equations with **Fractions**

Multiply <u>every term</u> of the equation by whatever's on the <u>bottom</u> of the fraction.

Example

Solve the equation $\frac{2}{5}(4z - 5) = 6$.

$$\frac{2}{5}(4z - 5) = 6$$

Start by <u>multiplying by 5</u> to get rid of the fraction.

(× 5) $\quad \frac{2}{5}(4z - 5) \times 5 = 6 \times 5$

Multiply out the brackets.

$$2(4z - 5) = 30$$
$$8z - 10 = 30$$

The opposite of −10 is +10, so <u>add 10</u> to both sides.

(+ 10) $\quad 8z - 10 + 10 = 30 + 10$
$$8z = 40$$

The opposite of ×8 is ÷8, so <u>divide both sides by 8</u>.

(÷ 8) $\quad 8z \div 8 = 40 \div 8$
$$z = 5$$

If there are two fractions with <u>different denominators</u>, you need to multiply by <u>both</u> denominators.

Example

Solve the equation $\frac{3x + 5}{2} = \frac{4x + 10}{3}$.

(× 2) (× 3) $\quad \dfrac{2 \times 3 \times (3x + 5)}{2} = \dfrac{2 \times 3 \times (4x + 10)}{3}$

Start by <u>multiplying by 2 and 3</u> to get rid of the fractions.

$$3(3x + 5) = 2(4x + 10)$$

Multiply out the brackets.

$$9x + 15 = 8x + 20$$

(− 8x) $\quad 9x + 15 - 8x = 8x + 20 - 8x$

To get the x's on only one side, <u>subtract 8x</u> from each side.

$$x + 15 = 20$$

(− 15) $\quad x + 15 - 15 = 20 - 15$

The opposite of +15 is −15, so <u>subtract 15</u> from both sides.

$$x = 5$$

Solving Simple **Quadratic Equations**

The <u>nastiest equation</u> you can expect in the exam is one with x^2 in it. If you end up with 'x^2 = a number' you can solve it by taking the <u>square roots</u> of each side. Remember that when you take the square root of a number the answer can be <u>positive</u> or <u>negative</u>.

Example

Solve $3x^2 = 12$.

$$3x^2 = 12$$

Divide both sides by 3.

(÷ 3) $\quad 3x^2 \div 3 = 12 \div 3$
$$x^2 = 4$$

Take square roots of both sides.

($\sqrt{\,}$) $\quad \sqrt{x^2} = \sqrt{4}$ so $x = 2$ or $x = -2$

Solve $x(x - 3) = 16 - 3x$.

$$x(x - 3) = 16 - 3x$$

Multiply out the brackets.

$$x^2 - 3x = 16 - 3x$$

Add 3x to both sides.

(+ 3x) $\quad x^2 - 3x + 3x = 16 - 3x + 3x$
$$x^2 = 16$$

Take square roots of both sides.

($\sqrt{\,}$) $\quad \sqrt{x^2} = \sqrt{16}$ so $x = 4$ or $x = -4$

Aim of the game — get the letter you want by itself...

1) Solve $\frac{1}{3}(3x - 5) = 1$.

2) Solve the equation $\frac{3 - x}{6} = \frac{x + 2}{2} - 1$.

3) Solve these equations: a) $x^2 = 9$ b) $x^2 + 5 = 30$ c) $x(2x + 1) = x + 2$

Using Expressions and Formulas

Expressions and formulas will come up over and over again, so make sure you're happy with them.

Substitute **Numbers** for **Letters**

You might be given an expression or formula and asked to work out its value when you put in certain numbers. All you have to do here is follow this method.

1) Write out the expression or formula.
2) Write it again, directly underneath, but substituting numbers for letters.
3) Work it out in stages. Use BODMAS (see p.3) to work things out in the right order. Write down values for each bit as you go along.
4) DO NOT attempt to do it all in one go on your calculator — you're more likely to make mistakes.

Example

Find the value of $3j - 2k$ when $j = 4$ and $k = -5$.

$3j - 2k$ ——————————— 1) Write out the expression.
$= 3 \times 4 - 2 \times -5$ ————— 2) Write it again, substituting numbers for letters.
$= 12 - -10 = 12 + 10 = 22$ —— 3) Work out the multiplications first, then do the subtraction.

Sometimes you might need to do a bit of solving to get your answer. Substitute the numbers in first, and then solve as usual.

Example

A formula used in physics is $s = ut + \frac{1}{2}at^2$. Work out the value of u if $s = 80$, $t = 5$ and $a = 4$.

$s = ut + \frac{1}{2}at^2$ ———————————— 1) Write out the formula.
$80 = (u \times 5) + (\frac{1}{2} \times 4 \times 5 \times 5)$ —— 2) Write it again, substituting numbers for letters.
$80 = 5u + 50$
$(-50) \quad 80 - 50 = 5u + 50 - 50$ ———— 3) Solve to find u.
$(\div 5) \quad 30 \div 5 = 5u \div 5$
$6 = u$, or $u = 6$

Rearrange to Change the **Subject** of a **Formula**

Rearranging formulas means making a different letter the subject — you have to get the subject on its own. You can use the same methods that you used for solving equations (see p.36-38).

Example

Rearrange $a = 2b - 3$ to make b the subject of the formula.

$a = 2b - 3$
$(+3) \quad a + 3 = 2b - 3 + 3$ — The opposite of -3 is $+3$, so add 3 to both sides.
$a + 3 = 2b$
Careful here — you divide the whole side by 2, not just one term.
$(\div 2) \quad (a + 3) \div 2 = 2b \div 2$ — The opposite of $\times 2$ is $\div 2$, so divide both sides by 2.
$\frac{a+3}{2} = b$ OR $b = \frac{a+3}{2}$

Work through the calculation one step at a time...

1) $C = 5a + 2b$. a) Find C when $a = 8$ and $b = 3$. b) Rearrange the formula to make a the subject.

Making Formulas from Words

Before getting started on formulas, make sure you can remember these definitions.

> EXPRESSION — a <u>collection</u> of <u>terms</u> (see p.32). Expressions <u>DON'T</u> have an = sign in them.
> EQUATION — an expression with an = sign in it (so you can solve it).
> FORMULA — a <u>rule</u> that helps you work something out (it will also have an = sign in it).

Making a **Formula** from **Given Information**

Making <u>formulas</u> from <u>words</u> can be a bit confusing as you're given a lot of <u>information</u> in one go. You just have to go through it slowly and carefully and <u>extract the maths</u> from it.

Example

Ruby is x years old. Alia is 3 years older than Ruby. Rohat is 5 times as old as Ruby.

a) **Write an expression for Alia's age in terms of x.**

Ruby's age is x.
So Alia's age is $x + 3$. — Alia is 3 years older, so add 3.

b) **Write an expression for Rohat's age in terms of x.**

Ruby's age is x. — 5 times older
So Rohat's age is $5 \times x = 5x$.

Example

The cooking time (T minutes) for a turkey is 40 minutes per kilogram (k), plus an extra 20 minutes. Write a formula for T in terms of k.

$$T = 40k + 20$$

A turkey with mass k will take $40 \times k$ minutes.

Don't forget to add on the extra time (20 minutes).

Because you're asked for a formula, you must include the '$T =$' bit (i.e. don't just put $40k + 20$).

Using Your **Formula** to **Solve Problems**

Sometimes, you might be asked to <u>write</u> a formula and use it to <u>solve a problem</u>.

Example

A mechanic charges £100 plus £50 for each part he replaces (R). Si gets a repair bill of £450. Write a formula for the total repair cost and use it to find how many parts were replaced on Si's car.

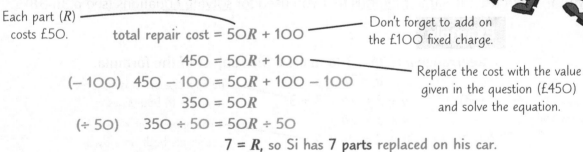

Each part (R) costs £50.

total repair cost $= 50R + 100$

Don't forget to add on the £100 fixed charge.

$450 = 50R + 100$

$(-100) \quad 450 - 100 = 50R + 100 - 100$

$350 = 50R$

$(\div 50) \quad 350 \div 50 = 50R \div 50$

Replace the cost with the value given in the question (£450) and solve the equation.

$7 = R$, so Si has **7 parts** replaced on his car.

Pick out the important maths bits and ignore the rest...

1) Hiring a canoe costs £8 per hour plus a £10 deposit. Lily paid £34. How long did she hire the canoe for?

Inequalities

Inequalities aren't too bad — you just have to find the values which make the statement true.

Using the **Inequality Symbols**

> means '<u>Greater than</u>'   ≥ means '<u>Greater than or equal to</u>'

< means '<u>Less than</u>'   ≤ means '<u>Less than or equal to</u>'

The one at the <u>BIG</u> end is <u>BIGGEST</u>, so $x > 4$ and $4 < x$ both mean: '<u>x is greater than 4</u>'.

Example

> Integers are just whole numbers (don't get caught out — O is neither positive or negative).

Write down all possible values of x in these inequalities.

a) **x is a positive integer such that $x \leq 3$.**

x is a <u>positive</u> integer that is <u>less than or equal to</u> 3:   1, 2, 3

b) **x is a negative integer such that $-5 < x$.**

x is a <u>negative</u> integer that is <u>greater than</u> –5:   –4, –3, –2, –1

Sometimes an inequality will contain <u>more than one</u> symbol. Here's how you tackle those ones.

Example

If x is an integer such that $-2 < x \leq 4$, write down all possible values of x.

Work out what <u>each bit</u> of the inequality is telling you:

$-2 < x$ means that x is greater than –2

$x \leq 4$ means that x is less than or equal to 4

Now just write down <u>all the values</u> that x can take: –1, 0, 1, 2, 3, 4

You Can Show Inequalities on **Number Lines**

Drawing inequalities on a <u>number line</u> is dead easy — all you have to remember is that you use an <u>open circle</u> (O) for > or < and a <u>coloured-in circle</u> (●) for ≥ or ≤.

Example

Show the inequality $-1 < x \leq 5$ on a number line.

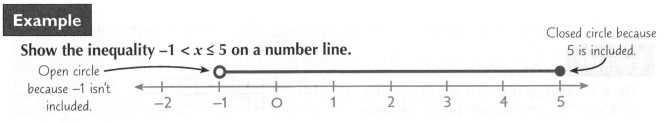

Open circle because –1 isn't included.

Closed circle because 5 is included.

An <u>arrow</u> simply means that the line keeps going on <u>forever</u>.

Example

Show the inequality $x > 4$ on a number line.

Open circle because 4 isn't included.

Arrow because it doesn't have a maximum value.

Maths > every other subject...

1) Write down all positive integers that satisfy the inequality $5 > x$.

2) Show the range of values that satisfies $x \geq 3$ on a number line.

 42

 42

42

 # Number Patterns and Sequences

Sequences are patterns of numbers or shapes that follow a rule — you need to spot what the rule is.

Finding Number Patterns

The trick to finding the rule for number patterns is to write down what you have to do to get from one number to the next in the gaps between the numbers. There are 2 main types to look out for:

1) Arithmetic sequences — Add or subtract the same number each time.

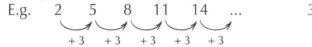

The RULE: 'Add 3 to the previous term'.   'Subtract 6 from the previous term'.

2) Geometric sequences — Multiply or divide by the same number each time.

The RULE: 'Multiply the previous term by 3'.   'Divide the previous term by 10'.

You might get number patterns that follow a different rule — for example, you might have to add or subtract a changing number each time, or you might get a sequence like the Fibonacci sequence (1, 1, 2, 3, 5, ...) where you add together the two previous terms. You just need to describe the pattern and use your rule to find the next terms.

Example

Find the next two terms in the sequence 1, 3, 6, 10, 15, ...

> This is the sequence of triangular numbers.

The rule is "increase the number you add by 1 each time". So the next two terms are 15 + 6 = 21 and 21 + 7 = 28.

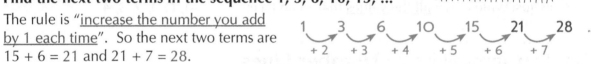

Shape Patterns

If you have a pattern of shapes, you need to be able to continue the pattern. You might also have to find the rule for the pattern to work out how many shapes there'll be in a later pattern.

Example

Here are some patterns made of squares.
a) Draw the next pattern in the sequence.
b) Work out how many squares there will be in the 6th pattern.

a) Just continue the pattern — add an extra square to each of the three legs.

b) Set up a table to find the rule:

Pattern number	1	2	3	4	5	6
Number of squares	1	4	7	10	13	16

The rule is 'add 3 to the previous term'. So just keep on adding 3 to extend the table until you get to the 6th term — which is 16.

Move over polka dots — there's a new pattern in town...

Remember, you always need to work out how to get from one term to the next — that's the rule.

1)   Find the rule and write down the next term in the sequence that starts 38, 32, 26, 20 ...

Section 2 — Algebra

Number Patterns and Sequences

Finding the Anything-th Term

You need to be able to find any term in a sequence without having to count all the way.
For sequences with a <u>common difference</u> — where you <u>add</u> or <u>subtract</u> the
<u>same number</u> each time, you can find the <u>term</u> from the <u>term number</u> like this.

Example

If the sequence is decreasing, the difference between each term will be negative.

Find the 40th term of the sequence that starts 5, 9, 13, 17, ...

term number: 1   2   3   4

term: 5   9   13   17

                + 4   + 4   + 4

1) Find the rule for getting the term from the term number by first finding the <u>difference</u> between each term. Here, it's <u>4</u>.

term number × 4:   4   8   12   16

                  +1   +1   +1   +1

term: 5   9   13   17

2) <u>Multiply</u> the <u>term number</u> by the <u>difference</u>.

3) Work out how to get from the <u>term number × 4</u> to the <u>corresponding term</u>.

The rule is multiply the term number by 4 and add 1.

4) Write down the rule and <u>check</u> it. (For term 3: $3 \times 4 + 1 = 13$ ✓)

So the 40th term is $40 \times 4 + 1 = \mathbf{161}$

5) Use the rule to find the <u>40th term</u>.

The nth Term

The *n*th term is an <u>expression</u> for the term with term number *n*. Here's how to find one.

Example

Find an expression for the *n*th term of the sequence that starts 2, 8, 14, 20, ...

n: 1   2   3   4

term: 2   8   14   20

         + 6   + 6   + 6

1) Find the <u>common difference</u>. It's <u>6</u>, so this tells you '<u>6n</u>' is in the formula.

2) List the values of <u>6n</u>.

$6n$:   6   12   18   24

        − 4   − 4   − 4   − 4

term: 2   8   14   20

3) Work out what you have to <u>add</u> or <u>subtract</u> to get from 6n to the term. So it's <u>−4</u>.

So the expression for the *n*th term is $\mathbf{6n - 4}$

4) Put '<u>6n</u>' and '<u>−4</u>' together.

Check your formula by putting the first few values of n back in:
$n = 1$: $6n - 4 = 6 - 4 = 2$ ✓ $n = 2$: $6n - 4 = 12 - 4 = 8$ ✓

Using the nth Term

Sometimes you'll be given the <u>rule</u> for a sequence and you have to work out what the 10th,
50th or <u>anything-th</u> term is. This method works for <u>any</u> type of sequence.

Example

What is the 40th term of the sequence given by the *n*th term rule $3n^2 + 4n + 10$?

1) Write out the expression. $3n^2 + 4n + 10$

2) Replace *n* with 40. $= 3 \times 40^2 + 4 \times 40 + 10$

3) Calculate using BODMAS. First do the <u>square</u>... $= 3 \times 1600 + 4 \times 40 + 10$

4) ...then the <u>multiplications</u> and finally the <u>addition</u>. $= 4800 + 160 + 10 = \mathbf{4970}$

Additional

That's terms covered — wait till you get to the conditions...

1) A sequence starts 15, 23, 31, ...   a) Find the rule to give any term.   b) Find the 28th term.

2) Write down a formula for the *n*th term of the sequence that starts 3, 15, 27, 39, ...

Simultaneous Equations

Simultaneous equations are two equations that you solve at the same time. The method of solving them is a little bit tricky. That's why there's a lovely six-step approach for you to learn. Follow it exactly and you'll be on to a winner.

Six Steps for Simultaneous Equations

Example

Solve the simultaneous equations $x = 3y - 10$ and $-2 + 2y = 3x$.

1) <u>Rearrange both equations</u> into the form <u>$ax + by = c$</u>, and label the two equations ① and ②.

    a, b and c are numbers (which can be negative).

$$x - 3y = -10 \quad - \quad ①$$
$$-3x + 2y = 2 \quad - \quad ②$$

2) <u>Match up the numbers in front</u> (the 'coefficients') of either the x's or y's in both equations. You may need to multiply one or both of them by a suitable number. Relabel them ③ and ④.

$$① \times 3: \quad 3x - 9y = -30 \quad - \quad ③$$
$$-3x + 2y = 2 \quad - \quad ②$$

<u>Multiply</u> every term in ① by 3 to get a 3 in front of the x.

3) <u>Add or subtract the two equations</u> to eliminate terms with the same number in front of x or y.

$$③ + ②: \quad 0x - 7y = -28$$

If the coefficients have <u>the same sign</u> (both +ve or both −ve) then <u>subtract</u>. If the coefficients have <u>opposite signs</u> (one +ve and one −ve) then <u>add</u>.

4) <u>Solve</u> the resulting equation.

$$-7y = -28$$
$$(\div -7) \quad -7y \div -7 = -28 \div -7$$
$$\underline{y = 4}$$

5) <u>Substitute</u> the value you've found back into equation ① and <u>solve</u> it to find the other value.

$$\text{Sub } y = 4 \text{ into } ①: \quad x - (3 \times 4) = -10$$
$$x - 12 = -10$$
$$(+ 12) \quad x - 12 + 12 = -10 + 12$$
$$\underline{x = 2}$$

6) <u>Substitute both</u> these values into equation ② to make sure it works. If it doesn't then you've done something wrong and you'll have to do it all again.

Sub x and y into ②: $(-3 \times 2) + (2 \times 4) = -6 + 8 = 2$, which is right, so it's worked.
So the solutions are: **$x = 2$, $y = 4$**

Remember to write out the pair of solutions clearly...

1) Find x and y when $x + 4y = 14$ and $6y - x = 6$.

2) At Di's Discs, CDs cost £x and DVDs cost £y. Jack bought 3 CDs and 2 DVDs and spent £26. Jill bought 4 CDs and 1 DVD and spent £23.

    a) Write two equations in terms of x and y to show how much Jack and Jill each spent.

    b) Solve these two equations simultaneously to find the cost of CDs and DVDs.

Warm-Up and Practice Questions

That's the algebra section all wrapped up, but the only way to know if you've taken it all in is with some good old-fashioned practice. Have a go at these questions and see how you get on.

Warm-Up Questions

1) Simplify: a) $x + x + y + y + y$ b) $5t + 7s - 2t - 12s$ c) $5b \times 3b \times 2$ d) $\dfrac{10a}{a}$

2) Multiply out and simplify: a) $3(4a + 2)$ b) $-6(2 - 3b)$ c) $5 - 3(z + 1)$

3) Factorise fully: a) $5x + 10$ b) $-3m - 12$ c) $6 - 9p^2$

4) Solve: a) $7x - 2 = 12$ b) $\dfrac{2x - 1}{2} = 3$ c) $3(x - 4) = 24$

5) $a = 3$, $b = -1$, $c = 4$. Find: a) abc b) $4a - 2b$ c) $(2b)^2 + \dfrac{c}{2}$

6) List all the integers that satisfy the inequality $-2 < x \le 5$.

7) What are the next two terms in each of the following sequences?
   a) 5, 12, 19, 26, ...   b) 16, 10, 4, –2, ...   c) 240, 120, 60, 30, ...

8) What is the nth term of the sequence that begins 7, 10, 13, 16, ...?

9) Find x and y given that $4x + y = 5$ and $2x - y = 7$.

Practice Questions

1) The diagram shows some floor patterns made up of shaded and unshaded square tiles.

pattern 1

pattern 2

pattern 3

a) Draw the fourth pattern on the blank grid below.

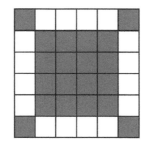

[1 mark]

b) How many black squares will be in the 5th pattern?

There will be a 5 by 5 square of shaded tiles in the middle, and 1 shaded tile in each corner.

$(5 \times 5) + 4 = 25 + 4 = 29$

.........29.........

[3 marks]

Practice Questions

2) Simplify:

   a) $6x - 4y - 7x + 5y$

....
[2 marks]

   b) $3a^2 \times 2ab$

....
[2 marks]

3) Multiply out the brackets and simplify:

   a) $3(5x - 1) + 2x$

....
[2 marks]

   b) $16 - 4(2a - 3)$

....
[2 marks]

   c) $4y^2 - y(5 - 2y)$

....
[2 marks]

4) Fully factorise:

   a) $6y - 3$

....
[2 marks]

   b) $8a + 28b$

....
[2 marks]

   c) $5a^2 - 10ab$

....
[2 marks]

Practice Questions

5) Show the inequality $1 < x \leq 7$ on a number line.

[2 marks]

6) Solve:

a) $4x + 7 = 15$

[2 marks]

b) $\dfrac{3x - 1}{5} = 4$

[2 marks]

c) $\dfrac{2x + 1}{3} - \dfrac{x - 3}{2} = 2$

Additional

[5 marks]

7) Find the 50th term of the following sequences.

a) 7, 9, 11, 13, …

[3 marks]

b) 11, 7, 3, –1, …

[3 marks]

Practice Questions

8) Jan thinks of a positive number. She doubles it, then adds 3. Then she squares the result.
   The answer is 81. What number is Jan thinking of?

   ....
   [3 marks]

9) The formula $V = \frac{1}{3}\pi r^2 h$ is used to calculate the volume of a cone.
   Rearrange the formula to make h the subject.

   ....
   [2 marks]

10) Solve the simultaneous equations $4x + 5y = 6$ and $2x = y - 4$.

   ....
   [5 marks]

Additional

Summary Questions

There was a lot of nasty algebra in that section — let's see how much you remember.
* Try these questions and tick off each one when you get it right.
* When you've done all the questions for a topic and are completely happy, tick off the topic.

Algebra (p.32-35) ☐

1) Simplify: a) $a + a + a + a$ b) $3b + 8b - 2b$ c) $d + 3e + 5d - 2e$ ☐
2) Simplify: a) $g \times g \times g$ b) $(ab)^2$ c) $(2mn)^3$ d) $\frac{6g}{24}$ ☐
3) Expand: a) $3(v + 8)$ b) $-7(2w + 5)$ ☐
4) Expand and simplify $4(3y - 4) - 2$.   ☐
5) Factorise fully: a) $3x + 9$ b) $7x + 21y$ ☐
6) Factorise fully: a) $5g^2 - 2g$ b) $6h + 12h^2$ c) $4jk^5 + 18j^3k$ ☐
7) Show that $4(5 - 2y) + 3(y - 10)$ can be written as $-5(y + 2)$.   ☐
8) Prove that $5x(x - 2) - x(5 - x)$ is a multiple of 3 for any integer value of x.   ☐

Solving Equations (p.36-38) ☐

9) Solve: a) $x + 12 = 19$ b) $2x = 14$ c) $3x + 5 = 14$ d) $\frac{x}{3} = 2$ ☐
10) Solve: a) $10 = 5x - 4$ b) $8(x - 2) = 4x$ c) $\frac{1}{4}(3x - 2) = 2x - 3$ ☐
11) Solve the equation $\frac{x-3}{5} = \frac{x-1}{4} - 1$.   ☐
12) Solve: a) $\frac{x^2}{2} = 18$ b) $x(x + 8) = 2(4x + 32)$ ☐

Formulas, Expressions and Inequalities (p.39-41) ☐

13) Work out the value of $4m + 7n$ when $m = -2$ and $n = 3$.   ☐
14) Find q if $p = 2q - 3$ and $p = 15$.   ☐
15) Rearrange the following formulas to make b the subject:
    a) $a = 3b + 2$ b) $a = \frac{1}{3}b - 7$ c) $a = \frac{5b - 1}{4}$ ☐
16) Bo goes shopping and buys s steaks (at £7 each) and f fish (at £4 each).
    He spends £P in total. Write a formula for P in terms of s and f.   ☐
17) Find all the possible positive integer values of x that satisfy: a) $x < 7$ b) $7 < x \leq 11$ ☐
18) Show the inequality $-4 < x < 4$ on a number line.   ☐

Number Patterns and Sequences (p.42-43) ☐

19) For each of the following sequences, find the next term and write down the rule you used.
    a) 2, 8, 14, 20, ...   b) 3, 9, 27, 81, ...   c) 95, 86, 77, 68, ...
    d) 1, 4, 9, 16, ...   e) 2, 3, 5, 8, 13, ...   f) 1, 8, 27, 64, ...   ☐
20) Write a rule to find any term of the sequence that starts 3, 9, 15, ... from the term number.   ☐
21) Find an expression for the nth term of the sequence that starts 5, 7, 9, 11, ...   ☐
22) Find the 6th term of the sequence with nth term $9n^2 + 1$.   ☐

Simultaneous Equations (p.44) ☐

23) Solve these equations simultaneously: $4x - y = 3$ and $3x + 2y = 16$ ☐

Section 2 — Algebra

X and Y Coordinates

What could be more fun than points in one quadrant? Points in four quadrants, that's what...

The Four **Quadrants**

A graph has <u>four different quadrants</u> (regions).

The top-right region is the easiest because <u>ALL THE COORDINATES IN IT ARE POSITIVE</u>.

You have to be careful in the <u>other regions</u> though, because the x- and y- coordinates could be <u>negative</u>, and that makes life much more difficult.

Three important points about coordinates:

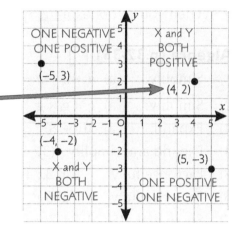

(x, y)

1) The coordinates are always in <u>ALPHABETICAL ORDER, x then y</u>.
2) x is always the flat axis going <u>ACROSS</u> the page.
   In other words '<u>x is a...cross</u>'. Get it — x is a '×'.
3) Remember it's always <u>IN THE HOUSE</u> (→) and then <u>UP THE STAIRS</u> (↑) so it's <u>ALONG first</u> and <u>then UP</u>, i.e. x-coordinate first, and then y-coordinate.

The **Midpoint** of a Line

The '<u>MIDPOINT OF A LINE SEGMENT</u>' is the <u>POINT THAT'S BANG IN THE MIDDLE</u> of the line.

Finding the <u>coordinates</u> of a midpoint is pretty easy. Just learn these <u>three steps</u>...

1) Find the <u>average</u> of the <u>x-coordinates</u>.
2) Find the <u>average</u> of the <u>y-coordinates</u>.
3) Put them in <u>brackets</u>.

Example

R and S have coordinates (1, 1) and (5, 6).
Find the midpoint of the line RS.

Average of x-coordinates = $\dfrac{1+5}{2}$ = 3

Average of y-coordinates = $\dfrac{1+6}{2}$ = 3.5

Coordinates of midpoint = **(3, 3.5)**

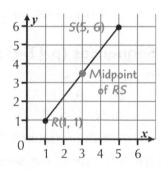

Xandy — a fun nickname for someone called Alexander...

1) Draw a coordinate grid for x and y from −8 to 8 and plot the points A(2, −4) and B(−7, 6).
2) M and N have coordinates (−4, 2) and (2, −1). Find the midpoint of the line MN.

Straight Line Graphs

Over the next few pages you'll get to see all sorts of straight lines. You're in for a treat.

Vertical and Horizontal Lines: 'x = a' and 'y = a'

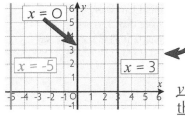

<u>$x = a$</u> is a <u>vertical line</u> through <u>'a'</u> on the x-axis

<u>$y = a$</u> is a <u>horizontal line</u> through <u>'a'</u> on the y-axis

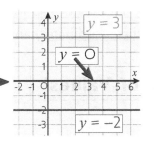

Remember — all the points on $x = 3$ have an <u>x-coordinate of 3</u>, and all the points on $y = 3$ have a <u>y-coordinate of 3</u>.

The Main Diagonals: 'y = x' and 'y = –x'

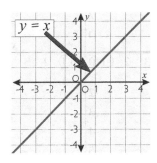

'<u>$y = x$</u>' is the <u>main diagonal</u> that goes <u>UPHILL</u> from left to right.

The x- and y-coordinates of each point are <u>the same</u>, e.g. (4, 4).

'<u>$y = -x$</u>' is the <u>main diagonal</u> that goes <u>DOWNHILL</u> from left to right.

The x- and y-coordinates of each point are <u>negatives of each other</u>, e.g. (–4, 4).

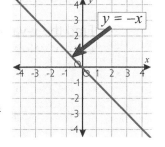

Other Lines Through the Origin: 'y = ax' and 'y = –ax'

<u>$y = ax$</u> and <u>$y = -ax$</u> are the equations for <u>A SLOPING LINE THROUGH THE ORIGIN</u>.

The value of '<u>a</u>' (known as the <u>gradient</u>) tells you the steepness of the line. The bigger 'a' is, the steeper the slope. A <u>MINUS SIGN</u> tells you it slopes <u>DOWNHILL</u>.

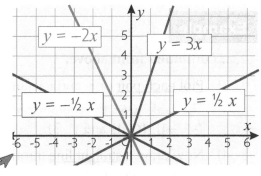

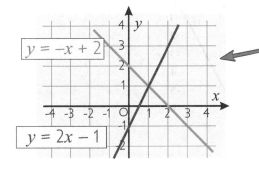

For a <u>sloping line</u> that <u>doesn't pass through the origin</u>, the equation of the line is <u>$y = mx + c$</u>. <u>m</u> is the <u>gradient</u> of the line and <u>c</u> is the <u>y-intercept</u> (where the line crosses the y-axis).

If an equation for a straight line isn't already in the form $y = mx + c$, you can rearrange the equation so it is.

A minus sign in front of the x term gives a downhill graph...

1) Point P has coordinates (2, 4). a) Which vertical line goes through point P?
   b) Which horizontal line goes through point P?

2) Describe what the line $y = -4x$ looks like.

Plotting Straight Line Graphs

It's likely you'll have to draw a straight line graph in the exam, so learn this method —
it'll lead you to the correct answer every time:

1) Choose <u>3 values of x</u> and <u>draw up a table</u>. ←
2) <u>Work out the corresponding y-values</u>.
3) <u>Plot the coordinates</u>, and <u>draw the line</u>.

> You might get lucky and be given a table to complete in the exam. Don't worry if it contains more than 3 values — just complete it all in the same way.

Doing the 'Table of Values'

Example

Draw the graph of $y = 2x + 1$ for values of x from −3 to 2.

1) <u>Choose 3 easy x-values for your table</u>:
Use x-values from the range you're given.
The question might give you the x-values.

x	−1	O	1
y			

2) <u>Find the y-values</u> by putting each x-value into the equation:

x	−1	O	1
y	−1	1	3

When $x = -1$,
$y = 2x + 1$
$= (2 \times -1) + 1 = -1$

When $x = 1$,
$y = 2x + 1 = (2 \times 1) + 1 = 3$

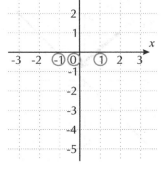

Plotting the Points and Drawing the Graph

Example

...continued from above.

3) <u>Plot each pair</u> of x- and y-values from your table.

The table gives the coordinates:
(−1, −1), (O, 1) and (1, 3).

4) Now draw a <u>straight line</u> through your points and label it with the <u>equation</u> of the line. Remember to extend the line through all the x-values given in the question.

> If one point looks a bit wacky, check 2 things:
> – the <u>y-value</u> you worked out in the table
> – that you've <u>plotted</u> it properly.

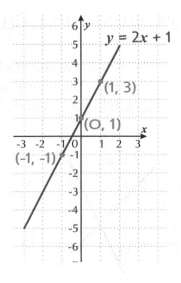

'Doing the table of values' sounds like a disco dance move...

When you choose the x-values to go in your table, make sure you choose sensible numbers.
You wouldn't want to end up doing calculations with numbers like 165 or 2.3657. Trust me.

1) a) Make a table of values for $y = -2x + 4$.
   b) Draw the graph of $y = -2x + 4$ for values of x from −2 to 2.

Plotting Straight Line Graphs

Here's another method you need to know for drawing straight line graphs.
Again, you find points on the line using the equation, but just two points this time.

Using the 'x = 0, y = 0' Method

1) Put $x = 0$ into the equation and find y — this is where it crosses the y-axis.
2) Put $y = 0$ into the equation and find x — this is where it crosses the x-axis.
3) Plot these two points and draw a straight line through them.

You can set x and y equal to other numbers, but using zero usually makes the maths easier.

Example

Draw and label the graph of $y = -3x + 6$ on the grid below.

1) It's a good idea to draw up a table of values for the two points. Fill in $x = 0$ for the first pair of coordinates and $y = 0$ for the second.

x	O	
y		O

2) Find the missing values by putting $x = 0$ and $y = 0$ into the equation.

x	O	2
y	6	O

$x = O$ gives:
$y = (-3 \times O) + 6$
$y = O + 6,$
so $y = 6$

$y = O$ gives:
$O = -3x + 6$
$3x = 6,$
so $x = 2$

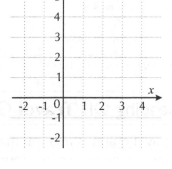

Once you've got your two points, just plot them as usual.

Example

...continued from above.

3) Plot both pairs of x- and y-values from your table.

The table gives the coordinates (O, 6) and (2, O).

One point should lie on the x-axis and the other should lie on the y-axis.

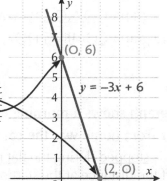
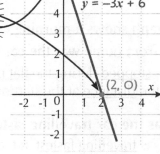

4) Finally draw a straight line through your points. Don't forget to label your line with its equation.

Make sure you double check you've plotted your points accurately — with just two points it's harder to spot mistakes.

Lines cross the y-axis when x = 0, and the x-axis when y = 0...

1) a) For the equation $y = 2x + 2$, find y when $x = 0$ and find x when $y = 0$.
   b) Use your answers to part a) to draw the graph of $y = 2x + 2$ for x from -3 to 3.

Reading Off Graphs

Here's a nice little page for you on reading graphs. At last, the graphs make themselves useful.

Getting Answers from a Graph

You can read values from a graph using this method:

> 1) <u>Draw a straight line</u> to the graph from <u>one axis</u>.
> 2) Then <u>draw a straight line</u> down or across to <u>the other axis</u>.

Example

Look at this graph of y against x.

a) **Find the value of x when $y = 5$.**

Draw a line <u>across from the y-axis</u> to the graph at $y = 5$ and then <u>down to the x-axis</u>. $x = 5$

b) **Find the value of y when $x = 3$.**

Draw a line <u>up from the x-axis</u> to the graph at $x = 3$ and then <u>across to the y-axis</u>.

$y \approx 3.3$

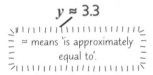 $\approx$ means 'is approximately equal to'.

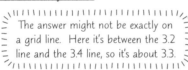 The answer might not be exactly on a grid line. Here it's between the 3.2 line and the 3.4 line, so it's about 3.3.

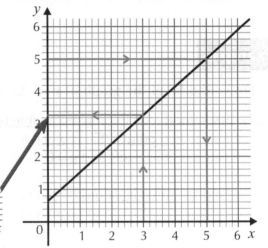

Reading Off Travel Graphs

A <u>travel graph</u> is a graph made up of <u>different straight lines</u>, showing the <u>stages</u> in a journey something makes.

1) A <u>TRAVEL GRAPH</u> is always <u>DISTANCE</u> (↑) against <u>TIME</u> (→).
2) <u>FLAT SECTIONS</u> are where it's <u>STOPPED</u>.
3) The <u>STEEPER</u> the graph the <u>FASTER</u> it's going.
4) The graph <u>GOING UP</u> means it's travelling <u>AWAY</u>.
5) The graph <u>COMING DOWN</u> means it's <u>COMING BACK AGAIN</u>.

Example

This travel graph shows a morning car journey.

a) **How far from home was the car the 2nd time it stopped?**

The car is <u>stopped</u> during the <u>flat parts</u> of the graph. <u>Read off</u> the <u>distance</u> at the start of the <u>2nd</u> flat section. **50 km**

b) **When was the car travelling fastest?**

The car was <u>travelling fastest</u> at the <u>steepest</u> part of the graph.

9 am to 9:30 am

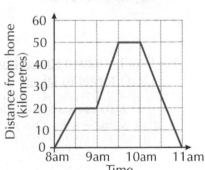

Draw lines on a graph with a ruler to help read off values...

1) Use the graph at the top of the page to find the value of y when $x = 2$.

Conversion Graphs

Yay, just what you wanted to see — more graphs...

Conversion Graphs

These are really easy if you remember the <u>method</u> for <u>reading graphs</u> on page 54.
Conversion graphs are used to <u>convert</u> between things like £ and dollars or mph and km/h, etc.

Example

The conversion graph below can be used to convert between miles and kilometres.

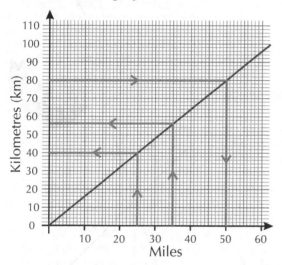

a) **Convert 25 miles into kilometres.**
   Draw a line <u>up</u> from 25 on the miles axis 'til it <u>hits the line</u>, then go <u>across</u> to the km axis.
   40 km

b) **Convert 80 kilometres into miles.**
   Draw a line <u>across</u> from 80 on the km axis 'til it <u>hits the line</u>, then go <u>down</u> to the miles axis.
   50 miles

c) **Find how many kilometres are equal to 35 miles.**
   The answer is 3 grid lines <u>above</u> 50 km, so you need to <u>work out</u> what the <u>scale</u> of the graph shows. Each <u>grid line</u> on the <u>y-axis</u> represents <u>2 km</u>.
   50 + (3 × 2) = 56 km

Drawing Your Own Conversion Graph

Exam questions sometimes ask you to <u>draw</u> the <u>conversion line</u> first — harsh, but true. You'll be given the information you need — use it to find at least <u>two points</u> to draw your straight line with.

Example

Martha has an old photograph. She knows its length in inches, but wants to convert the length into centimetres.

a) **Using 4 inches = 10 cm, draw a line on the graph to convert lengths up to 6 inches into centimetres.**

   Work out the coordinates of <u>two points</u> on the line and draw a <u>straight line</u> through them.

   4 inches = 10 cm, so one point is <u>(4, 10)</u>. Another easy point is <u>(0, 0)</u>.

b) **Martha's photograph has a length of 5 inches. Find the length in centimetres.**

   Draw a line <u>up</u> from <u>5 inches</u> to the line, then go <u>across</u> to the <u>centimetres</u> axis. **12.5 cm**

Make sure you show your working lines clearly.

Use a conversion graph to convert in either direction...

1) Use the conversion graph at the bottom of the page to convert 5 cm into inches.

Solving Simultaneous Equations

Solving simultaneous equations is just a mathsy way of saying "solving two equations at the same time". You can solve them using algebra (see p.44), or by drawing their graphs.

Solving **Simultaneous Equations** Using Graphs

To solve <u>two equations simultaneously</u>, you need to find values of <u>x and y</u> that make <u>both equations true</u>. Luckily there's an easy way to find them.

The <u>solution</u> of two simultaneous equations is simply the x- and y-values <u>where their graphs cross</u>.

Here's the general <u>method</u> to follow:

1) <u>Draw</u> the two graphs.

2) Find the <u>x- and y-values</u> where they <u>cross</u>.

3) Put the values back into <u>both equations</u> to check they work.

> The point where the lines cross is called the point of intersection.

Example

Use this graph to solve the equations $y = 3x + 1$ and $y = 5 - x$ simultaneously.

> The graphs are drawn for you so jump straight to step 2.

Find the <u>x-value</u> and the <u>y-value</u> where the <u>two lines cross</u>.

$x = 1$
$y = 4$

<u>Check</u> the values — put the <u>x-value</u> into each equation and check it gives you the correct <u>y-value</u>.

$y = (3 \times 1) + 1 = 4$ ✓
$y = 5 - 1 = 4$ ✓

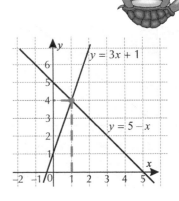

Exam questions might take you through the method in <u>stages</u>.

Example

Using the grid opposite:

a) **Draw the graph of $x - y = -1$ by completing this table of values.**
Find the <u>missing values</u> by putting $x = 0$ and $y = 0$ into the equation.
Then <u>plot</u> the points and <u>draw the line</u>.

x	0	−1
y	1	0

b) **Draw the graph of $4x + y = 6$ by completing this table of values.**
Find the <u>missing values</u> by putting $x = 0$ and $y = 2$ into the equation.
Then <u>plot</u> the points and <u>draw the line</u>.

x	0	1
y	6	2

> This y-value makes the numbers easy.

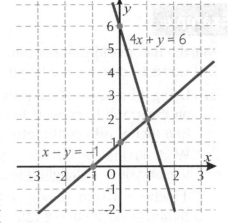

c) **Write down the solution to the equations $x - y = -1$ and $4x + y = 6$.**
Read off the <u>x- and y-values</u> where the <u>lines cross</u> and <u>check</u> they work.

$x = 1$ $y = 2$
$1 - 2 = -1$ ✓ $(4 \times 1) + 2 = 6$ ✓

I prefer simultaneous eating, like popcorn and chocolate...

1) a) Draw the graphs of $y = 2x - 2$ and $y = 4 - x$ on the same axes.

   b) Solve the simultaneous equations $y = 2x - 2$ and $y = 4 - x$.

Quadratic and Reciprocal Graphs

These graphs have lovely smooth curves — more of a test for your graph-drawing skills.

Drawing Quadratic and Reciprocal Graphs

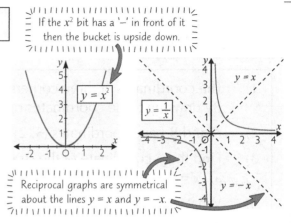

1) Quadratic graphs are of the form y = anything with x^2 (but not higher powers of x). They all have the same symmetrical bucket shape, called a parabola.

2) Reciprocal graphs are of the form $y = \frac{A}{x}$, where A is just a number. They appear as two symmetrical curves — one in the top right, one in the bottom left.

Example

Complete the table of values for the equation $y = \frac{6}{x}$ and then draw the graph.

x	−6	−3	−2	−1	1	2	3	6
y	−1	−2	−3	−6	6	3	2	1

1) Work out each y-value by substituting the corresponding x-value into the equation.

$x = -2$: $y = \frac{6}{-2} = -3$

$x = 1$: $y = \frac{6}{1} = 6$

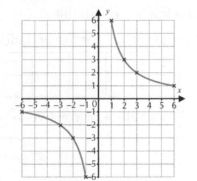

2) Plot the points and join them up to form two smooth curves. Definitely DON'T use a ruler.

NEVER EVER let one point drag your line off in some ridiculous direction. When a graph is generated from an equation, you never get spikes or lumps — only MISTAKES.

Using Quadratics or Reciprocals to Solve Simultaneous Equations

A quadratic or reciprocal and a straight line graph can cross at two points (two points of intersection). These points are the solutions to the simultaneous equations shown on the graph.

Example

This graph shows the curve $y = x^2 - 2x$.

a) On the same axes, draw and label the graph of the straight line with equation $y = 2x + 5$.

1) Fill in a table of values.
2) Plot the points and draw the straight line.

x	−2	0	2
y	1	5	9

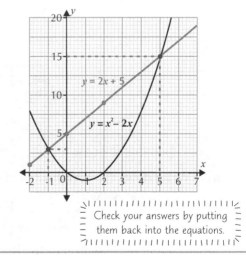

b) Use your graph to solve the simultaneous equations $y = x^2 - 2x$ and $y = 2x + 5$.

The line crosses the curve at (−1, 3) and (5, 15).
So your solutions are: $x = -1$, $y = 3$ and $x = 5$, $y = 15$

Check your answers by putting them back into the equations.

These graphs should be as smooth as a baby's bottom...

1) a) Draw the graphs of $y = x^2 + 3$ and $y = 2x + 6$ on a set of axes with x from −3 to 3.
   b) Write down the solutions to the simultaneous equations $y = x^2 + 3$ and $y = 2x + 6$.

Warm-Up and Practice Questions

It's not quite time to wave goodbye to graphs just yet. First you'll need to have a go at these warm-up and practice questions to see how much you've understood from the past few pages.

Warm-Up Questions

1) The coordinates of three corners of a rectangle are (0, 0), (5, 0) and (0, 10).
    By drawing these coordinates on a graph, find the coordinates of the fourth corner.

2) A and B have coordinates (3, 2) and (3, 8). Find the midpoint of the line AB.

3) Find the y-coordinate of the straight line given by the equation $y = -3x + 5$ when:
    a) $x = 0$ b) $x = 10$ c) $x = -50$ d) $x = 100$

4) What is always plotted up the vertical axis of a travel graph?

5) A rental car costs £90 to hire for a week and £10 for each additional day.
    Draw a graph to show the cost of a rental car for up to 15 days.

6) If two simultaneous equations are drawn on a graph, how do you find the solution?

7) How can you tell if an equation is a quadratic?

8) a) Complete the table of values below for the equation $y = \dfrac{8}{x}$.

x	−8	−4	−2	−1	1	2	4	8
y				−8		4		

   b) Draw the graph of $y = \dfrac{8}{x}$ for values of x between −8 and 8.

Additional

Practice Questions

1) The points A, B and C are shown on the graph below.

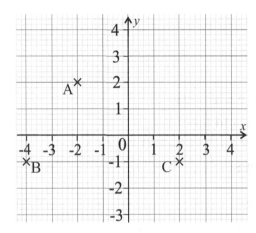

   a) Write down the coordinates of A, B and C.

   A = ...(−2, 2).........   B = ...(−4, −1).........   C = ...(2, −1).........

   [3 marks]

   b) What is the equation of the line BC?

   A horizontal line through −1.

   ....$y = -1$.........

   [1 mark]

Practice Questions

2) The travel graph on the right shows the journey
    of a woman who's running in a race.

    a) How far does she run in
        the first 15 minutes?

        ....
        [1 mark]

    b) Between which two times was the woman
        running slowest?

        ....
        [2 marks]

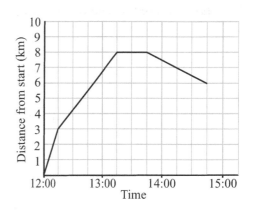

3) The graph on the left shows how the number
    of bacteria in a colony changed over time.

    a) How many bacteria were
        there after 5 days?

        ....
        [2 marks]

    b) How long was it before there
        were 100 000 bacteria?

        ....
        [2 marks]

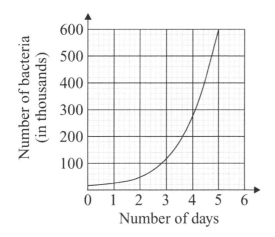

4) a) Plot the graph of $y = 2x + 3$
        on the grid on the right.

        [3 marks]

    b) On the same grid draw the line $y = 5$.

        [1 mark]

    c) Write down the coordinates of the point
        where these two lines meet.

        ....
        [1 mark]

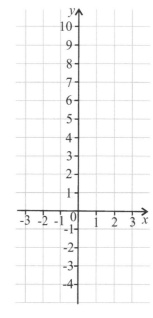

Practice Questions

5) The graph below can be used to convert pounds into US dollars ($).

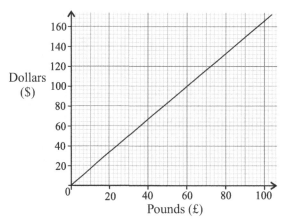

a) Estimate how much £50 is in dollars.

....

[2 marks]

b) Estimate how much $500 is in pounds.

....

[3 marks]

6) Look at the diagram below. Use it to solve the following simultaneous equations.

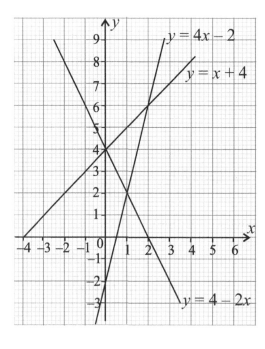

a) $y = x + 4$ $y = 4x - 2$ $x =$ .... $y =$ ....

[1 mark]

b) $y = x + 4$ $y = 4 - 2x$ $x =$ .... $y =$ ....

[1 mark]

61

Practice Questions

7) a) On the grid below, draw and label the graph of the equation $y = 2x + 1$.

[3 marks]

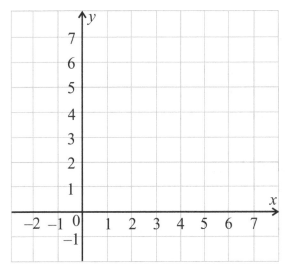

b) On the grid, draw and label the graph of the equation $x + y = 7$.

[3 marks]

c) Use the graphs you have drawn for a) and b) to find the values of x and y which satisfy the simultaneous equations $y = 2x + 1$ and $x + y = 7$.

$x =$ .... $y =$ ....
[1 mark]

Additional

8) a) On the grid, plot points for $y = 2x^2 - 10$ and join them up to form a smooth curve.

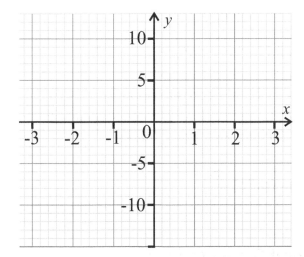

[4 marks]

b) Use your graph to solve $2x^2 - 10 = 2x - 2$, giving your answers to 1 d.p.

....
[5 marks]

Section 3 — Graphs

62

Summary Questions

Well, that wraps up Section 3 — time to test yourself and find out how much you really know.
- Try these questions and tick off each one when you get it right.
- When you've done all the questions for a topic and are completely happy, tick off the topic.

Coordinates (p.50) ☐

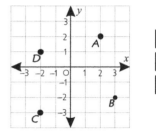

1) Give the coordinates of points A to D in the diagram on the right. ☐
2) Find the midpoint of a line segment with endpoints C and D. ☐
3) Find the midpoint of a line segment with endpoints A and B. ☐

Straight Line Graphs (p.51) ☐

4) Give the coordinates of one point on each of these lines: a) $x = 4$ b) $y = 2$ ☐
5) Write down the coordinates of the point where the lines $x = 3$ and $y = 1$ intersect. ☐
6) Write down two equations that give vertical lines. ☐
7) Say whether the graphs of these equations go uphill, downhill or neither (from left to right):
   a) $y = -2$ b) $y = -3x$ ☐

Plotting Straight Line Graphs (p.52-53) ☐

8) Draw the graph of $y = -3x + 2$ for the values of x from -2 to 2. ☐
9) For the equation $y = -2x + 10$, find y when $x = 0$ and x when $y = 0$.
   Use your answers to draw the graph of $y = -2x + 10$ for values of x from -5 to 5. ☐

Reading Off Graphs (p.54-55) ☐

10) Describe the general method for reading values from a graph. ☐
11) The graph on the right shows Bob's bicycle journey
    to the shop and back.
    a) Did he ride faster on his way to the
       shop or on his way home?
    b) How long did he spend in the shop? ☐

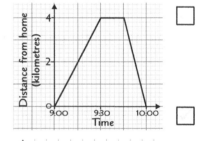

12) Use the conversion graph opposite to convert:
    a) 250 pounds to euros   b) 600 euros to pounds ☐
13) For a test that is marked out of 20, draw a conversion graph
    to convert marks up to 20 into percentage marks. ☐

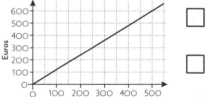

Simultaneous Equations (p.56) ☐

14) By drawing the graphs of $y = 2x$ and $y = x + 2$, solve the equations simultaneously. ☐

Quadratic and Reciprocal Graphs (p.57) ☐

15) What is the general shape of a reciprocal graph? ☐
16) a) Make a table of values for the equation $y = x^2 - 3$ for values of x between -3 and 3.
    b) Use your table in part a) to draw the graph of $y = x^2 - 3$.
    c) On the same axes draw the graph of $y = -x + 3$.
    d) Use your graphs to solve $y = x^2 - 3$ and $y = -x + 3$ simultaneously. ☐

Section 3 — Graphs

Ratios

Ratios can be a bit nasty, but the examples on the next few pages should cut them down to size.

Reducing **Ratios** to Their **Simplest Form**

To reduce a ratio to a simpler form, divide all the numbers in the ratio by the same thing (a bit like simplifying a fraction). It's in its simplest form when you can't divide anymore to get whole numbers.

Example

Vicky has 25 pork pies and Jonny has 15 pork pies. Write the number of Vicky's pies to Jonny's as a ratio in its simplest form.

1) First, write the numbers as a ratio.   25:15

2) Simplify the ratio — both numbers have a factor of 5, so divide them by 5. $\div 5 \binom{25:15}{} \div 5$
   We can't reduce this any further, so the simplest form of 25:15 is 5:3.   = 5:3

The More **Awkward Cases**

1) If the ratio contains decimals or fractions — multiply until you reach a whole number, then simplify.

   E.g. To simplify:
   $\times 10 \binom{1.2:1.5}{} \times 10$
   = 12:15
   $= \div 3 \binom{}{4:5} \div 3$

   $\frac{5}{6} : \frac{1}{2} : \frac{2}{3}$
   $\times 6 \binom{}{\downarrow \times 6} \times 6$
   = 5 : 3 : 4

2) If the ratio has mixed units — convert to the smaller unit before simplifying.

   E.g. To simplify: 18 mm:3.6 cm
   = 18 mm:36 mm
   $= \div 18 \searrow 1:2 \swarrow \div 18$

   If the units are the same, you can remove them.

3) To get to the form 1:n or n:1 — just divide. Decimals are okay in this case.

   #### Example

   Reduce 4:30 to the form 1:n.

   Divide both sides by 4: $\div 4 \binom{4:30}{} \div 4$
   = 1:7.5

   This form is often the most useful, since it shows the ratio very clearly.

   #### Example

   Write the ratio 1.2 kg:200 g in the form n:1.

   Convert 1.2 kg to 1200 g.
   Divide both sides by 200:   1200:200
   $\div 200 \binom{}{} \div 200$
   = 6:1

Simplifying a ratio is just like simplifying a fraction...

There are lots of different examples on this page, but the method for simplifying them is the same.

1) Simplify the following ratios: a) 7:63   b) 2.2:5.5   c) 8 cm:48 mm

Ratios

Ratios are so exciting (and important) that I decided they needed another page...

Scaling Up Ratios

If you know the <u>ratio between parts</u> and the actual size of <u>one part</u>,
you can <u>scale the ratio up</u> to find the other parts.

Example

Purple paint is made from red paint and blue paint in the ratio 5:3.

a) **If 20 pots of red paint are used, how much blue paint is needed?**

You need to <u>multiply by 4</u> to go from 5 to 20 on
the left-hand side (LHS) — so do that to <u>both sides</u>:

So **12 pots** of blue paint are needed.

red paint:blue paint

$= \quad \times 4 \overset{\curvearrowright}{(} 5:3 \overset{\curvearrowright}{)} \times 4$

$= \qquad 20:12$

b) **If 20 pots of red paint are used, how many pots of paint are used in total?**

Add the number of red and blue pots together.   20 + 12 = **32 pots**

Ratios with <u>3 parts</u> follow exactly the same rules:

Example

Brenda has a tray of cupcakes, scones and biscuits in the ratio 2:4:6. If she has 18 biscuits on the tray, how many cupcakes, scones and biscuits does she have in total?

1) Multiply <u>each number</u> in the
ratio by 3 to go from 6 to 18
on the right hand side (RHS).

cupcakes:scones:biscuits

$= \quad \times 3 \overset{}{(} 2 \; : \; 4 \; : \; 6 \overset{}{)} \times 3$
$\qquad \qquad \quad \downarrow \times 3$
$= \qquad 6 \; : \; 12 \; : \; 18$

2) <u>Add together</u> the numbers of
cupcakes, scones and biscuits.

6 + 12 + 18 = **36 cupcakes, scones and biscuits**

Writing a Fraction as a Ratio

You can rewrite <u>fractions</u> as <u>ratios</u> instead.

Example

Micaela owns a collection of 24 hats. $\frac{5}{8}$ of the hats are red and the rest are blue. What is the ratio of red hats to blue hats?

1) In every <u>8 hats</u>, 5 hats are red and 8 − 5 = 3 hats are blue.
2) So there are <u>5 red hats</u> for every <u>3 blue hats</u>.
   Write as a ratio: **Ratio of red to blue hats is 5:3.**

Ratios and fractions, on the same page? I'm spoiling you...

1) A fruit punch is made from orange juice and apple juice in the ratio 4:7.
   If 20 litres of orange juice is used, how much apple juice is used?

2) The ratio of first class to economy class passengers on a flight is 2:12.
   If there are 108 economy class passengers, how many passengers are there in total?

3) In an office, $\frac{3}{7}$ of the staff are men. What is the ratio of women to men in this office?

Ratios

... and another page. These examples are really important, so make sure you understand them.

Proportional **Division**

In a proportional division question a TOTAL AMOUNT is split into PARTS in a certain ratio.
The key word here is PARTS — concentrate on 'parts' and it all becomes quite painless.

Example

If Kim and Chris share £600 in the ratio 4:11, how much does Chris get?

1) ADD UP THE PARTS:
The ratio 4:11 means there will be a total of 15 parts: 4 + 11 = 15 parts

2) DIVIDE TO FIND ONE "PART":
Just divide the total amount by the number of parts: £600 ÷ 15 = £40 (= 1 part)

3) MULTIPLY TO FIND THE AMOUNTS:
We want to know Chris's share, which is 11 parts: 11 parts = 11 × £40 = **£440**

Example

Shauna and Roberto have 80 sweets between them.
Shauna has 4 times as many sweets as Roberto. How many sweets do they each have?

1) Work out the ratio.   Shauna has 4 sweets for every 1 that Roberto has, so the ratio is 4:1.

2) DIVIDE the TOTAL AMOUNT   There are 4 + 1 = 5 parts.
by the number of PARTS.   80 ÷ 5 = 16 (= 1 part)

3) Work out each person's share: Roberto has 1 part, so he has **16 sweets.**
Shauna has 4 parts, so she has 4 × 16 = **64 sweets.**

Check this by making sure they add up to 80. 16 + 64 = 80

Part:**Whole** Ratios

For part:whole ratios, the left hand side of the ratio is included in the right hand side.

Example

Mrs Miggins owns some tabby cats and ginger cats.
The ratio of tabby cats to the total number of cats is 3:5.

a) **What fraction of Mrs Miggins' cats are tabby cats?**
The ratio tells you that for every 5 cats, 3 are tabby cats. $\frac{part}{whole} = \frac{3}{5}$

b) **What is the ratio of tabby cats to ginger cats?**
3 in every 5 cats are tabby, so 2 in every 5 are ginger.   5 − 3 = 2
For every 3 tabby cats, there are 2 ginger cats.   tabby:ginger = **3:2**

If you're given a part:part ratio, you'll need to add up the total number of parts first.

c) **Mrs Miggins has 35 cats in total. How many ginger cats does she have?**
1) Find the total number of parts: 5 parts
2) Divide the total by the number of parts: 35 ÷ 5 parts = 7 (= 1 part)
3) Multiply to find the number of ginger cats, which is 2 parts: 2 parts = 2 × 7 = **14**

Time to get this part-y started...

1) Ahmed gets a share of a £500 prize. How much money will
Ahmed get if the ratio of his share to the total amount is 12:25?

Direct Proportion

Direct proportions aren't that bad really. Just learn the golden rule and all will be just fine.

Solving Direct Proportion Questions

Direct proportions tell you how <u>one thing increases</u> as <u>another increases</u> at the same rate. The <u>ratio</u> between the two things <u>stays the same</u>.

Two things are in direct proportion if, when you plot them on a graph, you get a straight line through the origin.

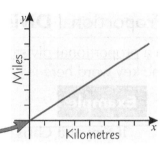

Remember, the <u>general equation</u> for a straight line through the origin is $\underline{y = Ax}$ (see p.51) where A is a constant (like 2 or 3). All direct proportions can be written as an equation in this form.

You can solve all direct proportion questions if you remember this <u>golden rule</u>:

> DIVIDE for ONE, then TIMES for ALL

Example

3 painters can paint 9 rooms per day.
How many rooms per day could 7 painters paint?

1) Start by <u>dividing by 3</u> to find how many rooms <u>1 painter</u> could paint per day.

$9 \div 3 = 3$ rooms per day

2) Then <u>multiply by 7</u> to find how many rooms <u>7 painters</u> could paint per day.

$3 \times 7 = 21$ rooms per day

Example

10 baguettes cost £1.50.

a) **How much will 12 baguettes cost?**
Start by <u>dividing by 10</u> to find the cost of <u>1 baguette</u>.   £1.50 ÷ 10 = £0.15
Then <u>multiply by 12</u> to find the cost of <u>12 baguettes</u>.   £0.15 × 12 = **£1.80**

b) **How many baguettes can be bought with £6?**
You know the cost of <u>1 baguette</u> from above.   £0.15
Just <u>divide</u> £6 by £0.15:   6 ÷ 0.15 = **40 baguettes**

Example

A recipe for 2 heaps of compost uses 1 kg of eggshells, 2 kg of manure and 3 kg of leaves. Work out the recipe for 5 heaps of compost.

1) Work out how much of each waste makes up 1 compost heap — <u>divide</u> each by <u>2</u>:

Eggshells: 1 ÷ 2 = 0.5 kg, Manure: 2 ÷ 2 = 1 kg, Leaves: 3 ÷ 2 = 1.5 kg

2) <u>Multiply</u> each type of waste by <u>5</u>:

Eggshells: 0.5 × 5 = **2.5 kg**, Manure: 1 × 5 = **5 kg**, Leaves: 1.5 × 5 = **7.5 kg**

Dividing for one is my favourite way to share cake...

1) 4 lumberjacks chop 12 trees in a day. How many trees could 13 lumberjacks chop in a day?

2) 15 koalas eat 7.5 kg of eucalyptus per day. How much eucalyptus do 18 koalas eat each day?

3) Mary's recipe to make 12 flapjacks requires 252 g oats, 120 g butter and 100 g sugar.
   Find the amounts of oats, butter and sugar needed to make 18 flapjacks.

    ☑   ☑   ☑

Inverse Proportion

Here's a trickier type of proportion — but once you've learnt this page you'll be an expert.

Solving Inverse Proportion Questions

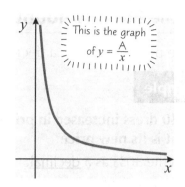

This is the graph of $y = \frac{A}{x}$.

When two things are in inverse proportion, one increases as the other decreases.

On the graph you can see that as the value of <u>x increases</u>, the value of <u>y decreases</u>. E.g. as the number of hours you watch TV increases, your score on a maths exam will decrease.

The general equation for inverse proportion is $y = \frac{A}{x}$ (see p.57).

On the previous page you saw the 'divide and times' method for solving direct proportions. Well, inverse proportions are the opposite so you have to:

> TIMES for ONE, then DIVIDE for ALL

Example

It takes 3 farmers 10 hours to plough a field. How long would it take 6 farmers?

Another way of looking at this question is that there are twice as many farmers, so it will take half as long (10 ÷ 2 = 5 hours).

1) Start by <u>multiplying by 3</u> to find how long it would take <u>1 farmer</u> to plough the field.

   10 × 3 = 30 hours for 1 farmer

2) Then <u>divide by 6</u> to find how long it would take <u>6 farmers</u> to plough the field.

   30 ÷ 6 = 5 hours for 6 farmers

Example

4 bakers can decorate 100 cakes in 5 hours.

a) How long would it take 10 bakers to decorate the same amount of cakes?

<u>Multiply by 4</u> to find how long it would take <u>1 baker</u>.   4 × 5 = 20 hours for 1 baker

<u>Divide by 10</u> to find how long it would take <u>10 bakers</u>.   20 ÷ 10 = **2 hours for 10 bakers**

b) Let b be the number of bakers and h be the time in hours it takes them to decorate 100 cakes. Write an equation in the form $h = \frac{A}{b}$ to represent this inverse proportion.

Find the <u>value of A</u> by putting <u>b = 4</u> and <u>h = 5</u> into the equation. $5 = \frac{A}{4}$ so A = 20

Put the <u>value of A</u> back into the equation. $h = \frac{20}{b}$

Inverse proportion — times for one and divide for all...

1) It takes 4 teachers 3 hours to mark all the Maths tests.
   How long would it have taken 6 teachers to mark all the Maths tests?

2) 3 cats eat a bag of cat food every 8 days.
   How long would it take 4 cats to eat a bag of cat food?

Percentage Change

Questions about percentage change are a bit trickier than finding basic percentages (see p.22).

Find the **New Amount** After a **% Increase or Decrease**

Turn the percentage into a <u>decimal</u>, then <u>multiply</u>. <u>Add</u> (or <u>subtract</u>) this on to the <u>original value</u>.

Example

A £40 dress increased in price by 30%.
What is its new price?

1) Write 30% as a <u>decimal</u>. $30 \div 100 = 0.3$

2) Find 30% <u>of</u> £40: $0.3 \times £40 = £12$

3) It's an increase, so <u>add</u> on
   to the original price: $£40 + £12 = £52$

Decrease 600 ml by 40%.

1) Write 40% as a decimal.
   $40 \div 100 = 0.4$

2) Find 40% <u>of</u> 600 ml.
   $0.4 \times 600 = 240$

3) It's a decrease, so <u>subtract</u>
   from the original volume:
   $600 - 240 = \textbf{360 ml}$

Finding the **Percentage Change**

This is the formula for giving a <u>change in value</u> as a <u>percentage</u> — <u>LEARN IT, AND USE IT</u>:

$$\text{Percentage 'Change'} = \frac{\text{'Change'}}{\text{Original}} \times 100$$

Typical questions will ask 'Find the percentage <u>increase</u> / <u>profit</u> / <u>error</u>' or
'Calculate the percentage <u>decrease</u> / <u>loss</u> / <u>discount</u>', etc.

Example

If a bus fare increases from £2.50 to £3, find the percentage increase.

1) Find the <u>actual increase</u> in price: increase $= £3 - £2.50 = £0.50$

2) Then use the <u>formula</u>:   percentage increase $= \frac{0.5}{2.5} \times 100 = \textbf{20\%}$

Example

The population of a village decreases from 800 to 680 people.
Find the percentage decrease of the village's population.

1) Find the <u>actual decrease</u> in population: decrease $= 800 - 680 = 120$

2) Then use the <u>formula</u>:   percentage decrease $= \frac{120}{800} \times 100 = \textbf{15\%}$

Add for a percentage increase, subtract for a decrease...

1) A company makes $12 000 profit in January and $21 000 profit in March.
   a) There is a 25% increase in profit from January to February. Find the profit for February.
   b) Calculate the percentage increase in profit from January to March.

2) A painting decreases in value from £8 million to £7.5 million. Find the percentage loss.

Percentage Change

Here's some more on percentage changes — it's a useful real-life skill so make sure you can do it.

Simple **Interest**

Sometimes, a certain percentage of an <u>original amount</u> is added at <u>regular intervals</u>, so the <u>same amount</u> is added <u>every time</u>. <u>Simple interest</u> is where a percentage of an original amount of <u>money</u> is added <u>every year</u>.

Example

Luna starts with £150 in her savings account. Each year, 2% of her original amount is added to her account. How much will she have in her savings account after 6 years?

1) Write 2% as a <u>decimal</u>. $2 \div 100 = 0.02$
2) <u>Multiply</u> 0.02 by £150 to find the money added <u>in 1 year</u>: $0.02 \times £150 = £3$
3) Multiply by 6 to get the <u>total amount</u> for <u>6 years</u>: $£3 \times 6 = £18$
4) It's an increase, so <u>add</u> on to the original amount: $£150 + £18 = \textbf{£168}$

Finding the **Original Value**

When you're given the <u>percentage change</u> and the <u>new value</u>, and you want the <u>original value</u>:

1) Write the amount in the question as a <u>percentage of the original value</u>.
2) <u>Divide</u> to find <u>1%</u> of the original value and <u>multiply by 100</u> to give the original value.

Example

John has a collection of vintage vehicles. Over a year, one car decreases in value by 40% to £7200, and one motorbike increases in value by 25% to £8750.

a) Calculate the original value of the car.

1) A <u>decrease</u> of 40% means £7200 represents <u>60% of the original</u> value.
2) Divide by 60 to find <u>1%</u> of the original value.
3) Then multiply by 100.

$$\div 60 \left\{ \begin{array}{l} £7200 = 60\% \\ £120 = 1\% \end{array} \right.$$
$$\times 100 \left\{ £12\ 000 = 100\% \right.$$

So the original value of the car was **£12 000**.

b) Calculate the original value of the motorbike.

1) An <u>increase</u> of 25% means £8750 represents <u>125% of the original</u> value.
2) Divide by 125 to find <u>1%</u> of the original value.
3) Then multiply by 100.

$$\div 125 \left\{ \begin{array}{l} £8750 = 125\% \\ £70 = 1\% \end{array} \right.$$
$$\times 100 \left\{ £7000 = 100\% \right.$$

So the original value of the motorbike was **£7000**.

Additional

Simple and interesting — what more could you want?..

1) Arabelle runs a distance of 1800 m. Each week, she increases the distance she runs by 15% of her original distance. What distance does she run after 5 weeks?
2) Radiators increase the temperature of a room by 25% to 22.5 °C. What was the temperature of the room before the radiators heated it up?

Metric and Imperial Units

There's nothing too bad on this page — just some facts to learn.

Metric Units

1) <u>Length</u>   mm, cm, m, km
2) <u>Area</u>   mm², cm², m², km², hectares
3) <u>Volume</u>   mm³, cm³, m³, ml, cl, litres
4) <u>Mass</u>   mg, g, kg, tonne
5) <u>Speed</u>   km/h, m/s
6) <u>Temperature</u>   °C

'Weight' is often used instead of 'mass' in everyday language.

MEMORISE THESE KEY FACTS:

1 cm = 10 mm	1 ml = 1 cm³
1 m = 100 cm	1 litre = 100 cl
1 km = 1000 m	1 gram = 1000 mg
1 litre = 1000 ml	1 kg = 1000 g
1 litre = 1000 cm³	1 tonne = 1000 kg

Imperial Units

1) <u>Length</u>   inches, feet, yards, miles
2) <u>Area</u>   square inches, square feet, square miles, acres
3) <u>Volume</u>   cubic inches, cubic feet, gallons, pints
4) <u>Mass</u>   ounces, pounds, stones, tons
5) <u>Speed</u>   mph
6) <u>Temperature</u>   °F

Don't panic — you don't need to learn these for your exam. But you should recognise the units.

IMPERIAL UNIT CONVERSIONS

1 foot = 12 inches
1 yard = 3 feet
1 gallon = 8 pints
1 stone = 14 pounds (lb)
1 pound = 16 ounces (oz)

Metric-Imperial Conversions

Make sure you learn these <u>approximate conversions</u>.
They'll help you change between <u>metric</u> units and <u>imperial</u> units.

'≈' means 'approximately equal to'.

APPROXIMATE CONVERSIONS

1 inch ≈ 2.5 cm	1 kg ≈ 2.2 pounds (lb)	1 foot ≈ 30 cm
1 litre ≈ 1.75 pints	1 mile ≈ 1.6 km (or 5 miles ≈ 8 km)	

3-Step Method for Converting

There are some examples of conversions on the next page.

① Find the <u>conversion factor</u> (always easy).

② Decide whether to <u>multiply</u> or <u>divide</u> by it
   (use the <u>conversion factor</u> to decide if the answer should be <u>bigger</u> or <u>smaller</u>).

③ <u>Work out</u> your answer (and <u>check it</u>).

No getting around it — you'll just have to memorise these...

The conversion factor in the 3-step method is just the number in the conversion, e.g. for
1 m = 100 cm, it's 100. If you don't know whether to multiply or divide by it, you can try both.

1) Convert: a) 3.5 cm to mm   b) 2.8 litres to cm³   c) 4.5 tonnes to kg.
2) Convert: a) 44 lbs to kg   b) 5 feet to cm   c) 20 km to miles.

Converting Units

Time to try out the 3-step method for converting (see p.70) — here are lots of fun examples.

Examples

Example

A zoo has a miniature gorilla called Augustus, who is 30 cm tall. How tall is he in m?

1) Find the <u>conversion factor</u>.

2) Decide whether to <u>multiply or divide</u> by it.

3) Work out the <u>answer</u>.

1 m = 100 cm, so conversion factor = 100

You'd expect more cm than m, so <u>divide</u>.

30 ÷ 100 = 0.3 m

Check your answer — 0.3 is less than 30, so this looks sensible.

Example

Nick lives 18 miles away from his friend Anna. Approximately, how far is this in km?

1) Find the <u>conversion factor</u>.

2) Decide whether to <u>multiply or divide</u> by it.

3) Work out the <u>answer</u>.

1 mile ≈ 1.6 km, so conversion factor = 1.6

You'd expect more km than miles, so <u>multiply</u>.

18 × 1.6 = 28.8, so **18 miles ≈ 28.8 km**

Check your answer — 28.8 is bigger than 18, so this looks sensible.

Example

Arjun owns 5 hectares of land. Use the conversion 1 hectare = 2.47 acres to work out the area of his land in acres. Give your answer to the nearest whole acre.

1) Find the <u>conversion factor</u> from the question.

2) <u>Decide</u> whether to <u>multiply or divide</u> by it.

3) Work out the <u>multiplication</u>.

4) Round your <u>answer</u>.

1 hectare = 2.47 acres, so conversion factor = 2.47

You'd expect more acres than hectares, so <u>multiply</u>.

5 × 2.47 = 12.35 acres.

Round 12.35 to the nearest acre = **12 acres**

Check your answer — 12 is bigger than 5, so this looks sensible.

Example

Write the following measurements in order of size from smallest to largest:
180 cm³, 1.75 litres, 185 ml

1) First, write all three measurements in the <u>same unit</u> — I'm going to choose cm³.

2) Write them out <u>in order</u>.

3) Convert back to the <u>original units</u>.

1 litre = 1000 cm³ and 1 ml = 1 cm³

So 1.75 litres = 1750 cm³ and 185 ml = 185 cm³

180 cm³, 185 cm³, 1750 cm³

180 cm³, 185 ml, 1.75 litres

You can use the same method for any unit conversion...

Always check your answer — if you end up with a ridiculously big or ridiculously small number, you probably multiplied when you should have divided or vice versa.

1) Write these measurements in order of size from smallest to largest: 44 mm, 0.5 m, 4.2 cm

2) Convert 26 miles into: a) kilometres   b) metres   c) centimetres

More Conversions

Converting areas and volumes from one unit to another is a bit treacherous,
because 1 m² does NOT equal 100 cm². Remember this and read on for why.

Converting **Area** and **Volume** Measurements

Be really <u>careful</u> — 1 m = 100 cm <u>DOES NOT</u> mean 1 m² = 100 cm² or 1 m³ = 100 cm³.
You won't slip up if you <u>LEARN THESE RULES</u>:

<u>Area</u>: units come with a <u>2</u>, e.g. mm², cm², m²
— <u>use the conversion factor 2 times</u>.

<u>Volume</u>: units come with a <u>3</u>, e.g. mm³, cm³, m³
— <u>use the conversion factor 3 times</u>.

$$1 \text{ m}^2 = 100 \text{ cm} \times 100 \text{ cm}$$
$$1 \text{ cm}^2 = 10 \text{ mm} \times 10 \text{ mm}$$

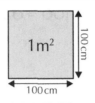

$$1 \text{ m}^3 = 100 \text{ cm} \times 100 \text{ cm} \times 100 \text{ cm}$$
$$1 \text{ cm}^3 = 10 \text{ mm} \times 10 \text{ mm} \times 10 \text{ mm}$$

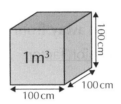

Example

Convert 5 m² to cm².
To change area measurements from
m² to cm², <u>multiply</u> by 100 <u>twice</u>.
5 × 100 × 100 = **50 000 cm²**

Convert 80 000 mm³ to cm³.
To change volume measurements from
mm³ to cm³, <u>divide</u> by 10 <u>three times</u>.
80 000 ÷ (10 × 10 × 10) = **80 cm³**

You should expect your answers to be <u>really big</u> or <u>really small</u> compared
to the value you're given — so if they're not, something's gone wrong.

Converting **Speeds**

To convert a speed, you might have to convert both <u>distance</u> and <u>time</u> units. Do it in <u>two stages</u>.

Example

**A panther at Birdingbury safari park was recorded running at 54 km/h.
How fast is this in metres per second?**

① First convert <u>54 km</u> into <u>m</u>:

1 km = 1000 m, so conversion factor = 1000
You'd expect more m than km, so multiply:
54 × 1000 = **54 000 m/h**

② Now convert <u>hours</u> into <u>seconds</u>.
Start with <u>hours</u> into <u>minutes</u>...

There are 60 minutes in an hour, so:
54 000 ÷ 60 = **900 m/minute**

You divide because the panther runs fewer metres per minute than per hour.

... then do <u>minutes</u> into <u>seconds</u>.

There are 60 seconds in a minute, so:
900 ÷ 60 = **15 m/s**

Once more, for luck — 1 m² is <u>not</u> equal to 100 cm²...

1) Convert: a) 2.4 cm³ into mm³   b) 400 000 cm² into m²
2) The speed limit along a stretch of road is 60 mph. What is this in km/h?

Reading Scales and Estimating

There's plenty of useful info to learn on this page — it may even come in handy in real life.

How to **Read** a **Scale**

All scales consist of a line divided into intervals. To read a point on the scale, you need to know what each small gap represents:

| Small gap | = | Size of large gap between numbers / Number of small gaps between numbers |

1) On the scale to the right, there's a difference of 10 between the numbers, and 5 small gaps between them, so each small gap is worth 10 ÷ 5 = 2 cm.

Large gap between numbers
0   10   20 Small gap 30   40

2) The orange arrow is 3 small gaps after 30 — 3 small gaps = 3 × 2 = 6, so it's pointing to 30 + 6 = 36 cm.

Example

Draw 148 km/h on this speedometer.

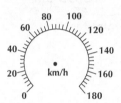

1) Work out what each small gap represents.

Large gap = 20
No. of small gaps = 5
Small gap = 20 ÷ 5 = 4 km/h

2) Find the nearest big number before 148. Then work out how many small gaps you need to add on.

140 + 4 = 144
144 + 4 = 148

So draw the arrow at 140 + 2 small gaps.

Choosing Units and **Estimating**

Think about what you're being asked to measure. Ask yourself if it's big or small — then choose the unit that'll give the most sensible answer.

Example

Choose the most sensible unit from the box on the right to measure:

metre	kilometre
centimetre	hectare
millilitre	litre
kilogram	gram

a) The volume of tea in a small mug.

Find the units used to measure volume. Litre, millilitre
Millilitres are smaller, so this is the most sensible unit. Millilitre

b) The mass of a hamster.

Find the units used to measure mass. Gram, kilogram
Grams are smaller, so this is the most sensible unit. Gram

Using sensible guesses you can also estimate the measurement of something.

Example

The man in the picture is 2 m tall. Estimate the height of the tree.

The tree is about one and a half times as tall as the man.

Rough height of tree = 1.5 × height of man
= 1.5 × 2 m = **3 m**

Reading scales — they're snakes from Berkshire...

1) How much liquid is there in this jug?

2) Which units from the box would you use to measure:
a) the length of a banana
b) the mass of a horse
c) the flight distance of a jumbo jet?

| mm | cm | tonnes | mg |
| g | km | kg | litres |

Section 4 — Ratio, Proportion and Rates of Change

Time

There's nothing new here — just a quick reminder about working with time.

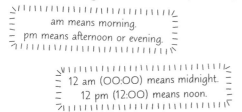

am means morning.
pm means afternoon or evening.

12 am (OO:OO) means midnight.
12 pm (12:OO) means noon.

12-hour clock	24-hour clock
12.00 am	00:00
5.12 am	05:12
4.15 pm	16:15

The hours on 12- and 24-hour clocks are different after 1 pm. To go from 12-hour to 24-hour add 12 hours, and subtract 12 to go the other way.

3.24 pm $\xrightarrow{+\ 12\ h}$ 15:24 $\xleftarrow{-\ 12\ h}$

Do **Time** Calculations in **Stages**

Be careful when using calculators in time calculations — the decimal answers they give are confusing, e.g. 2.5 hours = 2 hours 30 mins, NOT 2 hours 50 mins.

Example

How many minutes are there between 7.20 pm and 10.05 pm?

1) Split the time between 7.20 pm and 10.05 pm into simple stages.

7.20 pm → 9.20 pm → 10.00 pm → 10.05 pm
+ 2 hours + 40 minutes + 5 minutes

2) Convert the hours to minutes.   2 hours = 2 × 60 = 120 minutes
3) Add to get the total minutes.   120 + 40 + 5 = **165 minutes**

Example

Amy got the train from Catbury at 15:32 and got off the train at Pigstead. Use the timetable on the right to find how long her journey took in hours and minutes.

Timetable			
Catbury	1532	1602	1632
Wolfham	1645	1715	1745
Pigstead	1745	1815	1845

1) Read off the timetable to find the time when she got off the train.   17:45

2) Split the time between 15:32 and 17:45 into simple stages:

15:32 → 17:32 → 17:45
2 hours + 13 minutes = **2 hours and 13 minutes**

Days, Months and **Years**

Remember, remember the 5th of November. And also all these other facts:
- There are 365 days, or 12 months, in a year. (But there are 366 days in a leap year.)
- There are 10 years in a decade, 100 years in a century and 1000 years in a millennium.

Example

How many years and months are there between 27th November 2026 and 27th July 2030?

1) Count the number of whole years between the two dates.
Nov. 2026 → Nov. 2027 → Nov. 2028 → Nov. 2029
1 year + 1 year + 1 year = 3 years

2) This takes you to 27th November 2029. 8 months
Now count the number of months. **3 years and 8 months**

30 days has September, April, June and November. All the rest have 31, except February alone, which has 28 days clear, and 29 in each leap year.

Split time calculations into stages to make it easier...

1) How many months and days are there between 23rd April 2027 and 5th August 2027?

Speed

To answer speed, distance and time questions, learn the formula and put in the numbers.

Speed = Distance ÷ Time

Speed is the distance travelled per unit time, e.g. the number of km per hour or metres per second.

$$\text{SPEED} = \frac{\text{DISTANCE}}{\text{TIME}} \qquad \text{TIME} = \frac{\text{DISTANCE}}{\text{SPEED}} \qquad \text{DISTANCE} = \text{SPEED} \times \text{TIME}$$

Here's a handy formula triangle for speed — think of the words SaD Times to help you remember the order of the letters (S^DT).

E.g. to get the formula for speed from the triangle, cover up S and you're left with $\frac{D}{T}$.

HOW DO YOU USE FORMULA TRIANGLES?

1) COVER UP the thing you want to find and WRITE DOWN what's left showing.

2) Now PUT IN THE VALUES for the other two things and WORK IT OUT.

Example

A car travels 90 miles at 60 mph. How long does this take?

Write down the formula for time, put in the values and calculate:

$$\text{time} = \frac{\text{distance}}{\text{speed}} = \frac{90 \text{ miles}}{60 \text{ mph}} = 1.5 \text{ hours} = 1 \text{ h } 30 \text{ mins}$$

Find the Average Speed of a Journey

A journey could have lots of different stages. Look at the total time from start to finish, and the total distance travelled. You can use these to work out the average speed for the whole journey.

Example

Dave is doing a sponsored walk. He starts at 9.00 am and walks for 2 hours 45 minutes at 4 km/h. After stopping to rest for 15 minutes, he jogs a further 9 km in 1 hour. Dave then decides to run the remaining 7 km, finishing the walk at 1.30 pm.

a) **How far did Dave walk in the first 2 hours 45 minutes?**

Write down the formula for distance, put in the values and calculate:

distance = speed × time
= 4 km/h × 2.75 hours = **11 km**

Convert hours and minutes into a decimal first.

b) **What was Dave's average speed, in km/h, for the whole walk?**

1) Use your answer from part a) to work out his total distance travelled.

11 km + 9 km + 7 km = 27 km

2) Work out the total time from start to finish.

9.00 am → 1.00 pm → 1.30 pm
+ 4 hrs + 30 min = 4 hrs 30 mins
= 4.5 hours

3) Now write down the formula for speed, put in the values and calculate.

$$\text{speed} = \frac{\text{distance}}{\text{time}} = \frac{27 \text{ km}}{4.5 \text{ hours}} = 6 \text{ km/h}$$

Learn this stuff if you want to go the speed × time...

1) a) Katie runs 5 km in 25 minutes. What is her speed in km/h?

b) Katie then runs 10 km in 35 minutes. What is her average speed for the whole journey?

Section 4 — Ratio, Proportion and Rates of Change

Warm-Up and Practice Questions

That's this section all wrapped up, but before you put your feet up and have a biscuit, try out your new ratio and proportion skills with these lovely warm-up and practice questions.

Warm-Up Questions

1) Simplify the following ratios:
   a) 4 : 20   b) 7.5 : 12.5   c) 150 ml : 1 litre

2) Reduce 4 : 18 to the form 1 : n.

3) Harry and Rosa share 40 sweets in the ratio 3 : 5. How many sweets does Rosa get?

4) It takes 40 minutes to wash a car. How long would it take to wash 4 cars?

5) A laptop has 20% off in a sale. Its original price was £500. What is its price in the sale?

6) £5000 is deposited in a bank account offering 3% simple interest. How much interest is earned in 5 years?

7) Put the following masses in order from smallest to biggest: 5.5 kg, 7000 g, 10 lb

8) A fish tank has a volume of 0.24 m³. What is the volume of the fish tank in cm³?

9) Choose a sensible unit to measure: a) the height of a house   b) the mass of a tiger

10) A film starts at 7.30 pm and finishes at 9.55 pm. How long was the film?

11) A cyclist rides for 45 minutes at a speed of 20 km/h. How far did they travel?

Practice Questions

1) Fred walks 5400 m in 72 minutes.

   a) What is his average speed in km/h?

   Distance in km = 5400 ÷ 1000 = 5.4 km
   Time in hours = 72 ÷ 60 = 1.2 hours

   Convert the distance and time into the units you need for the answer — km and hours.

   Speed = $\frac{distance}{time}$ = $\frac{5.4}{1.2}$ = 4.5 km/h

   4.5 km/h
   [5 marks]

   b) How far will he travel in 48 minutes at this speed?

   Time in hours = 48 ÷ 60 = 0.8 hours
   Distance = speed × time = 4.5 × 0.8 = 3.6 km

   3.6 km
   [4 marks]

   c) If he kept at the same speed and had travelled 14 km and 400 m by the end of the day, how long had he been walking, in hours and minutes?

   Time = $\frac{distance}{speed}$ = $\frac{14.4}{4.5}$ = 3.2 hours

   Don't forget to convert your answer into hours and minutes.

   3.2 hours = 3 hours and (0.2 × 60) = 12 minutes

   3 hours and 12 minutes
   [4 marks]

Practice Questions

2)

6   8

    a)   Write down the number that the arrow is pointing at on the number line above.

                                                            ....
[1 mark]

    b)   Draw an arrow pointing at 6.4 on the number line above.

[1 mark]

3)   Alice has bought 14 calculators for £35. How much would 22 calculators cost?

                                                            ....
[2 marks]

4)   Reduce the following ratios to their simplest form:
    a)   15 : 20

                                                            ....
[2 marks]

    b)   8 cm : 32 mm

                                                            ....
[2 marks]

    c)   16 : 12 : 24

                                                            ....
[2 marks]

5)   Convert the following measurements:
    a)   7.2 litres into millilitres

                                                            ....
[1 mark]

    b)   60 000 cm^2 into m^2

                                                            ....
[2 marks]

Practice Questions

6) Shaun, Ben and David share 50 badges in the ratio $5:3:2$. How many badges does Shaun get?

....
[3 marks]

7) A salad dressing is made from olive oil and vinegar in the ratio $4:1$.
   a) How much vinegar is needed to make a salad dressing using 600 ml of olive oil?

....
[2 marks]

   b) How many litres of olive oil are there in 1.25 litres of salad dressing?

....
[3 marks]

8) In 2015, a Chocca chocolate bar weighed 60 g. In 2021, a Chocca bar weighed 51 g.
   Calculate the percentage decrease in the weight of a Chocca bar between 2015 and 2021.

....
[2 marks]

Practice Questions

9) A 500 ml bottle of orange juice costs £1.50. A 1.2 litre bottle of orange juice costs £3.40.
    Which bottle of orange juice is the best value for money?

    ....
    [3 marks]

10) 2 people take 8 hours to paint a mural.
    How long would it take 5 people to paint the same mural?

    ....
    [2 marks]

11) A sunflower is 165 cm tall. It is 20% taller than it was last week.
    How tall was the sunflower last week?

    ....
    [4 marks]

12) A remote control car travels at 7 m/s for 35 metres,
    then travels another 100 metres in 10 seconds.
    What is the average speed, in m/s, of the remote control car over the whole journey?

    ....
    [4 marks]

Summary Questions

Just when you thought you were done with Section 4, some sneaky revision questions appeared.
- Try these questions and <u>tick off each one</u> when you <u>get it right</u>.
- When you've done <u>all the questions</u> for a topic and are <u>completely happy</u>, tick off the topic.

<u>Ratios, Proportion and Percentage Change (p.63-69)</u> ☐

1) Reduce these ratios to their simplest form:
   a) 14:16   b) 27:18   c) 56 cm:0.49 m ☐

2) Write the ratio 5:18 in the form 1:n. ☐

3) Ria's DVD collection is made up of comedies, dramas and horror films only in the ratio 8:11:6, and she has 22 dramas. How many DVDs does she have in total? ☐

4) If Isla and Brett share £150 between them in the ratio 7:3, how much does Isla get? ☐

5) 18 sweets cost 90p. How much would 25 sweets cost? ☐

6) It takes 2 people 30 minutes to wrap 12 presents. How long would it take:
   a) 4 people to wrap 12 presents?   b) 2 people to wrap 24 presents? ☐

7) Ayoola's £200 pogo stick has decreased in price by 65%. How much is it worth now? ☐

8) If a train ticket increases from £5.00 to £5.80, what is the percentage increase? ☐

<u>Units and Conversions (p.70-72)</u> ☐

9) Write down the conversion factors used to convert between the following units:
   a) metres and kilometres   b) centimetres and inches   c) litres and pints ☐

10) A giant watermelon weighs 10 kg. What is this in grams? ☐

11) Convert the following: a) 80 km to miles   b) 2.5 feet to cm ☐

12) Convert the following: a) 20 cm into m   b) 6000 mm^2 into cm^2 ☐

13) A matchbox has a volume of 180 cm^3. What is its volume in mm^3? ☐

14) Charlotte is driving at 27 mph. What is her speed in km/h? ☐

<u>Reading Scales, Estimating and Time (p.73-74)</u> ☐

15) What measurement is the scale on the right showing?

16) What metric units would you use to measure the mass of a kiwi fruit? ☐

17) Estimate the volume of a milk carton. Choose from these options: 1 ml, 1 cl, 1 litre. ☐

18) How many minutes are there between 6.40 pm and 11.20 pm? ☐

<u>Speed (p.75)</u> ☐

19) Ramin cycles for 3 hours at a speed of 25 km/h. How far does he cycle? ☐

20) A tricycle takes 45 minutes to travel 3 km. How fast does it travel in km/h? ☐

21) Mariam rows 2 km in 30 minutes. The wind changes direction, and she rows a further 3 km at 10 km/h. What is her average speed for the whole distance she rows? ☐

Symmetry

There are two types of symmetry you need to know — line symmetry and rotational symmetry.

Line Symmetry

This is where you draw one or more <u>MIRROR LINES</u> across a shape and both sides will <u>fold exactly</u> together.

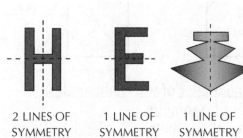 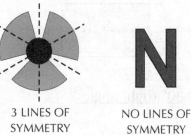

| 2 LINES OF SYMMETRY | 1 LINE OF SYMMETRY | 1 LINE OF SYMMETRY | 3 LINES OF SYMMETRY | NO LINES OF SYMMETRY | 1 LINE OF SYMMETRY |

Example

Shade two squares on the pattern on the right to make a pattern with two lines of symmetry, and draw on the lines of symmetry.

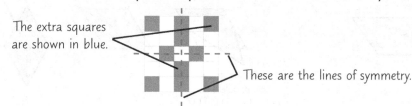

The extra squares are shown in blue.

These are the lines of symmetry.

Rotational Symmetry

This is where you can <u>rotate</u> the shape into different positions that <u>look exactly the same</u>.

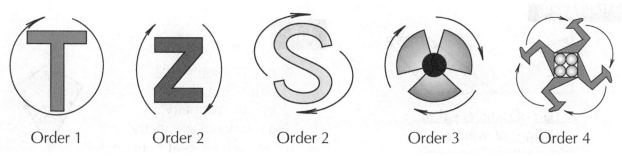

Order 1   Order 2   Order 2   Order 3   Order 4

The <u>ORDER OF ROTATIONAL SYMMETRY</u> is the posh way of saying: 'how many different positions look the same'. You should say the Z-shape above has '<u>rotational symmetry of order 2</u>'.

> When a shape has only 1 position you can either say that it has 'rotational symmetry of order 1' or that it has 'NO rotational symmetry'.

Before you turn the page, take some time to reflect...

1) How many lines of symmetry does the T-shape above have?
2) What is the order of rotational symmetry of the H-shape above?

Quadrilaterals

This page is full of quadrilateral facts that you'll need to learn.

Quadrilaterals (Four-Sided Shapes)

Rectangle
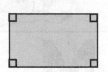

<u>4 equal angles</u> of <u>90°</u> (<u>right angles</u>)
<u>2 lines</u> of symmetry
rotational symmetry of <u>order 2</u>

Square
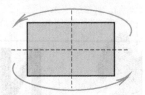

The little square means it's a right angle

<u>4 equal angles</u> of <u>90°</u> (<u>right angles</u>)
<u>4 lines</u> of symmetry,
rotational symmetry of <u>order 4</u>
Diagonals cross at <u>right angles</u>

Parallelogram (a rectangle pushed over)
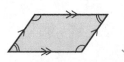
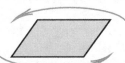

<u>2 pairs</u> of <u>equal sides</u>
(each pair are <u>parallel</u>)
<u>2 pairs</u> of <u>equal angles</u>
<u>NO lines</u> of symmetry,
rotational symmetry of <u>order 2</u>

Rhombus (a square pushed over)
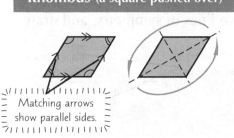
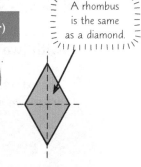

A rhombus is the same as a diamond.

Matching arrows show parallel sides.

<u>4 equal sides</u> (opposite sides are <u>parallel</u>)
<u>2 pairs</u> of <u>equal angles</u>
<u>2 lines</u> of symmetry,
rotational symmetry of <u>order 2</u>
Diagonals cross at <u>right angles</u>

Trapezium
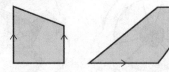

<u>1 pair</u> of <u>parallel sides</u>.
<u>NO lines</u> of symmetry*
No rotational symmetry

Kite
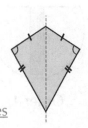

<u>2 pairs</u> of <u>equal sides</u>
<u>1 pair</u> of <u>equal angles</u>
<u>1 line</u> of symmetry
No rotational symmetry
Diagonals cross at <u>right angles</u>

*except for an <u>isosceles trapezium</u> (a trapezium where the non-parallel sides are the <u>same length</u>), which has <u>1 line</u> of symmetry.
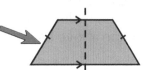

Quadrilaterals are one big four-sided family...

1) I am thinking of a shape with four sides. It has 2 pairs of equal sides and its diagonals cross at right angles. It has no rotational symmetry. What is the name of the shape I'm thinking of?

Triangles and Regular Polygons

There are some more 2D shapes coming up on this page — let's start off with triangles.

Triangles (Three-Sided Shapes)

Equilateral Triangles

3 equal sides and
3 equal angles of 60°
3 lines of symmetry,
rotational symmetry
of order 3 (see p.81)

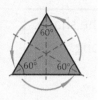

Right-Angled Triangles

1 right angle (90°)
No lines of symmetry
(unless it's an isosceles
right-angled triangle)

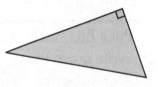

Scalene Triangles

All three sides different
All three angles different
No symmetry (pretty obviously)

Isosceles Triangles

2 sides the same
2 angles the same
1 line of symmetry
No rotational symmetry

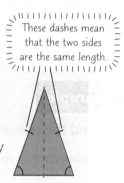

These dashes mean that the two sides are the same length.

Regular Polygons

A polygon is a many-sided shape. A regular polygon is one where all the sides and angles are the same. The regular polygons are a never-ending series of shapes with some fancy features.

EQUILATERAL TRIANGLE
3 sides
3 lines of symmetry
Rotational symmetry of order 3

SQUARE
4 sides
4 lines of symmetry
Rotational symmetry of order 4

REGULAR PENTAGON
5 sides
5 lines of symmetry
Rotational symmetry of order 5

REGULAR HEXAGON
6 sides
6 lines of symmetry
Rotational symmetry of order 6

REGULAR HEPTAGON
7 sides
7 lines of symmetry
Rotational symmetry of order 7
(A 50p piece is like a heptagon.)

REGULAR OCTAGON
8 sides
8 lines of symmetry
Rotational symmetry of order 8

REGULAR NONAGON
9 sides
9 lines of symmetry
Rotational symmetry of order 9

REGULAR DECAGON
10 sides
10 lines of symmetry
Rotational symmetry of order 10

Regular polygons have equal sides and equal angles...

1) A regular polygon has 20 sides. How many lines of symmetry does it have?
What is its order of rotational symmetry?

Perimeter and Area

Finding the perimeter is pretty straightforward if you use the big blob method.

Perimeter — **Distance** Around the **Edge** of a Shape

To find a perimeter, you add up the lengths of all the sides,
but the only reliable way to make sure you get all the sides is this:

1) Put a BIG BLOB at one corner and then go around the shape.
2) Write down the LENGTH of every side as you go along.
3) Even sides that seem to have NO LENGTH GIVEN
   — you must work them out.
4) Keep going until you get back to the BIG BLOB.
5) ADD UP all the lengths you've written down.

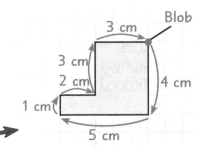

Example

Find the perimeter of the shape drawn on the grid. Each grid square represents 1 cm².

Perimeter = 4 + 5 + 1 + 2 + 3 + 3 = **18 cm**

Four **Area Formulas**

Area of RECTANGLE = length × width

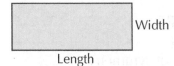

$$A = l \times w$$

Area of TRIANGLE = $\frac{1}{2}$ × base × vertical height

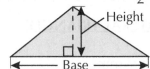

$$A = \frac{1}{2} \times b \times h$$

Area of PARALLELOGRAM = base × vertical height

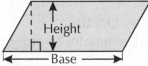

$$A = b \times h$$

Area of TRAPEZIUM = average of parallel sides × vertical height

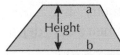

$$A = \frac{1}{2} \times (a + b) \times h$$

1) Height always means the vertical height, not the sloping height.
2) Remember that area is measured in square units (e.g. cm², m² or km²).

Example

Find the area of triangle A.

Use the formula: Area = $\frac{1}{2}$ × 18 × 12 = 9 × 12 = **108 cm²**

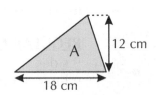

Learn the four area formulas — you won't regret it...

1) A rectangle has a perimeter of 14 m, and an area of 12 m². Write down its length and width.
2) Find the area of a parallelogram with a base of 8 cm and a height of 5 cm
   using the formula $A = b \times h$.

Area of Compound Shapes

Make sure you know how to find the area of different shapes — you'll need to do it again here.

Areas of **More Complicated** Shapes

You sometimes have to find the area of <u>strange-looking</u> shapes. What you always find with these questions is that you can break the shape up into <u>simpler ones</u> that you can deal with.

> 1) <u>SPLIT THEM UP</u> into the basic shapes: <u>RECTANGLES</u>, <u>TRIANGLES</u>, etc.
> 2) Work out the area of each bit <u>SEPARATELY</u>.
> 3) Then <u>ADD THEM ALL TOGETHER</u>.

Example

The shape of a symmetrical school badge is shown on the right. Find the area of the badge.

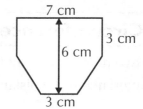

1) You need to work out the <u>area</u> of the badge — so split it into two shapes (a <u>rectangle</u> and a <u>trapezium</u>):

2) Find the area of the <u>rectangle</u>:

Area = $l \times w$ = 7 × 3 = 21 cm^2

3) Find the area of the <u>trapezium</u>:

Area = $\frac{1}{2} \times (a + b) \times h$

$= \frac{1}{2} \times (7 + 3) \times 3$

$= 5 \times 3 = 15$ cm^2

4) Add up the parts to find the <u>total area</u>: The total area of the badge is 21 + 15 = **36 cm^2**

Example

Maira has a parallelogram-shaped pond in her garden. If the shaded area of the diagram represents grass, calculate the area of the grass Maira has in her garden.

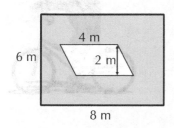

1) Find the area of the <u>whole garden</u>:

Area = $l \times w$ = 8 × 6 = 48 m^2

2) Find the area of the <u>pond</u>:

Area of parallelogram = $b \times h$ = 4 × 2 = 8 m^2

3) <u>Subtract</u> the pond area from the garden area.

Area of grass = 48 − 8 = **40 m^2**

Don't forget to add up the separate areas at the end...

As long as you know the area formulas, there's nothing on this page to trip you up. Here's a question to see if you've got it all down.

1) Find the area of the shape on the right.

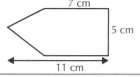

Circles

There's a surprising number of circle terms you need to know — don't mix them up.

Radius and Diameter

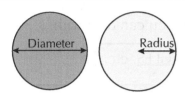

The <u>DIAMETER</u> goes <u>right across</u> the circle, passing through the <u>centre</u>.
The <u>RADIUS</u> goes from the <u>centre</u> of the circle to any point on the <u>edge</u>.

The <u>DIAMETER IS EXACTLY DOUBLE THE RADIUS</u>

E.g. if the radius is 4 cm, the diameter is 8 cm,
and if the diameter is 24 m, the radius is 12 m.

Area, Circumference and π

There are two more important formulas for you to <u>learn</u> — <u>circumference</u> and <u>area</u> of a circle.
The circumference is the distance round the outside of the circle (its <u>perimeter</u>).

1) <u>CIRCUMFERENCE</u> $= \pi \times$ diameter
$= \pi \times$ radius $\times 2$

$$C = \pi \times D \text{ or } C = 2 \times \pi \times r$$

2) <u>AREA</u> $= \pi \times (\text{radius})^2$

$$A = \pi \times r^2$$

$\pi = 3.141592.... = \underline{3.142}$ (approx)

The big thing to remember is that π (called "pi")
is just an <u>ordinary number</u> equal to 3.14159... or
3.142 rounded off. You can just use the π button
on your calculator (which is way more accurate).

So a circle with radius <u>4 cm</u> has a <u>circumference</u> of $2 \times \pi \times r = 2 \times \pi \times 4 = \underline{25.1 \text{ cm}}$ (1 d.p.)
and an <u>area</u> of $\pi \times r^2 = \pi \times 4^2 = \underline{50.3 \text{ cm}^2}$ (1 d.p.).

Finding the Radius or Diameter

You could be given the <u>circumference</u> or the <u>area</u> of a circle and asked
to find the <u>radius</u> or <u>diameter</u>. You do this by <u>using</u> the formulas above.

Example

**A circle has a circumference of 37.7 cm. What is its radius?
Write your answer to the nearest whole number.**

1) Write out the formula for <u>circumference</u>. $C = 2 \times \pi \times r$

2) <u>Substitute</u> the values that you know... $37.7 = 2 \times \pi \times r$

3) ...and <u>solve</u> to calculate r. $r = \dfrac{37.7}{2\pi} = 6.00014... = \textbf{6 cm}$

It takes about 3.14 chefs to bake the perfect pi...

1) Find the circumference and area (to 1 d.p.) of a circle with a diameter of 20 mm.

2) A circle has an area of 60 cm². Give its diameter to 3 significant figures.

Circle Problems

Here's some more circle stuff to get your head around.

Tangents, Chords, Arcs, Sectors and Segments

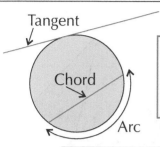

A TANGENT is a straight line that <u>just touches</u> the <u>outside</u> of a circle.
A CHORD is a line drawn <u>across the inside</u> of a circle.
AN ARC is just <u>part of the circumference</u> of a circle.

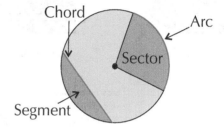

A SECTOR is a wedge-shaped area (like a slice of cake) cut right from the centre.
SEGMENTS are the areas you get when you cut a circle with a chord.

Finding the Area of a Sector

Finding the area of a <u>sector</u> can be a bit tricky — but there's a handy formula to help.

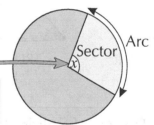

$$\text{AREA OF SECTOR} = \frac{x}{360} \times \text{Area of Full Circle}$$

$$\text{LENGTH OF ARC} = \frac{x}{360} \times \text{Circumference of Full Circle}$$

Example

Nick cuts a slice from a circular pizza with a radius of 9 cm.
The pizza remaining is shown in the diagram.
Work out the area of the remaining pizza to 1 d.p.

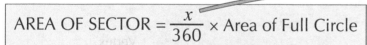

1) Start by working out the area of the <u>circle</u>. $A = \pi \times r^2 = \pi \times 9^2$
$= \underline{254.469...} \text{ cm}^2$

2) Now work out the area of the missing <u>sector</u> (the slice that's been removed). Area of sector $= \frac{50}{360} \times 254.469... = \underline{35.342...} \text{ cm}^2$

3) <u>Subtract</u> the area of the <u>sector</u> from the circle... $254.469... - 35.342... = \underline{219.126...} \text{ cm}^2$

4) ...and <u>round</u> your answer to 1 d.p.   So area of remaining pizza = **219.1 cm² to 1 d.p.**

Circles may be pointless, but this page certainly isn't...

1) Draw and label a circle with a chord, tangent and segment.

2) Find the area and perimeter of the shape to the right. Give your answers to 2 d.p.

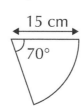

3) Work out the shaded area below. Give your answer to 1 d.p.

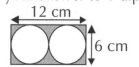

3D Shapes

3D shapes can be quite complicated, but luckily you don't need to know anything too tricky.

Eight **Solids** to Learn

3D shapes are solid shapes. These are some of the more common ones:

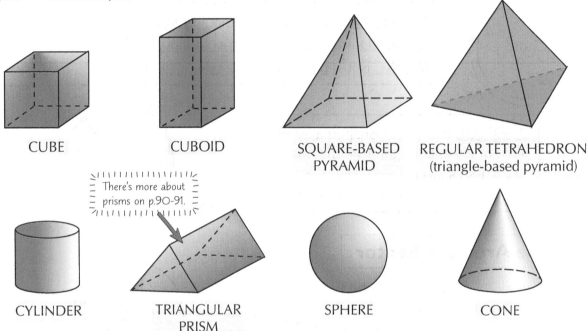

CUBE   CUBOID   SQUARE-BASED   REGULAR TETRAHEDRON
                           PYRAMID   (triangle-based pyramid)

There's more about prisms on p.90-91.

CYLINDER   TRIANGULAR   SPHERE   CONE
               PRISM

Different Parts of Solids

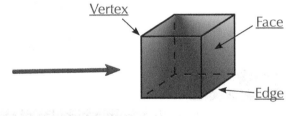

Vertex   Face

Edge

There are different parts of 3D shapes to know about.
These are vertices (corners), faces (the flat bits) and edges.

Example

For the cuboid on the right, write down the number of faces, the number of edges and the number of vertices.

A cuboid has 6 faces (don't forget the hidden faces — one on the bottom and two at the back shown by the dotted lines).

It has 12 edges (again, there are some hidden ones — the dotted lines in the diagram).

It has 8 vertices (one is hidden).

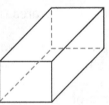

Example

Write down the number of faces on a triangular prism.

A triangular prism has 5 faces (there's one on the bottom and two at the back that you can't see).

It's one vertex but two vertices...

1) a) Write down the name of the shape on the right.
   b) How many faces and edges does it have?

Nets and Surface Area

Pencils and rulers at the ready — you might get to do some drawing over the next two pages.

Nets and Surface Area

1) A <u>NET</u> is just a hollow <u>3D shape</u> folded out flat.
2) There's often <u>more than one</u> net that can be drawn for a 3D shape (see the <u>cubes</u> below).
3) If you're given a net, you can <u>fold it up</u> to make a <u>3D shape</u>.
4) <u>SURFACE AREA</u> only applies to 3D objects — it's the <u>total area</u> of all the <u>faces</u> added together.
5) To find the surface area, sketch the <u>net</u>, then find the <u>area</u> of the net.

> Remember — <u>SURFACE AREA OF SOLID = AREA OF NET</u>.

Cubes

Nets of Cubes

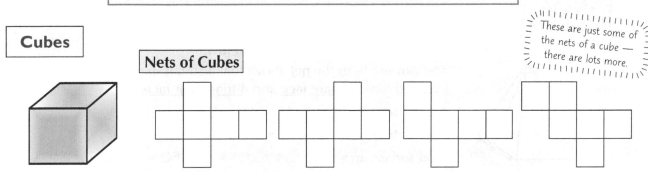

These are just some of the nets of a cube — there are lots more.

Cuboids

Net of Cuboid

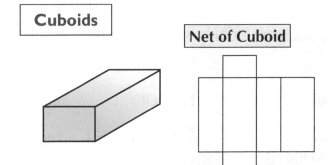

Notice that the net of a cuboid is made up of <u>3 different sized</u> rectangles (there are <u>2 of each size</u>). This is helpful when you're working out the <u>surface area</u>.

Example

Find the surface area of this cuboid:

Sketch the <u>net</u> of the shape, and label all the <u>measurements</u>:

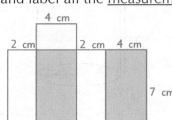

7 cm

2 cm

4 cm

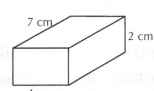

Then work out the <u>area</u> of <u>each face</u> and <u>add them up</u> (note there are 2 each of 3 different rectangles).

Surface area = 2(2 × 7) + 2(4 × 7) + 2(4 × 2)
= 28 + 56 + 16 = **100 cm²**

To see if you drew the net right, imagine folding it back up...

1) Find the surface area of a cube with side length 4 cm.

Nets and Surface Area

Another page on nets and surface area — it's time for prisms, pyramids and cylinders.

Prisms and Pyramids

Triangular Prism

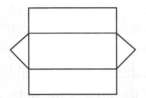

Net of triangular prism

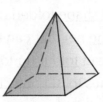

Square-Based Pyramid

Net of square-based pyramid

Example

> *Have a look back at p.84 for more on areas.*

Find the surface area of the square-based pyramid below.

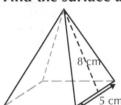

You can see from the <u>net</u> above that a square-based pyramid has <u>1 square face</u> and <u>4 triangular faces</u>.

Area of square face = 5 × 5 = 25 cm²

Area of triangular face = ½ × 5 × 8 = 20 cm²

Total surface area = 25 + (4 × 20) = 25 + 80 = **105 cm²**

Cylinders

<u>Cylinders</u> are a bit trickier — it's probably best to just <u>learn the formula</u> and stick the numbers in.

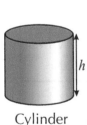

Cylinder

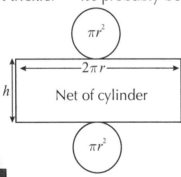

Net of cylinder

Surface area of a CYLINDER = $2\pi rh + 2\pi r^2$

Note that <u>the length of the rectangle</u> is equal to the <u>circumference</u> of the circular ends.

Example

Find the surface area of the cylinder to the right to 1 d.p.

Just put the <u>measurements</u> into the <u>formula</u>:

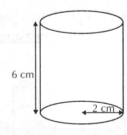

Surface area of cylinder = $2\pi rh + 2\pi r^2$
= $(2 \times \pi \times 2 \times 6) + (2 \times \pi \times 2^2)$
= 75.398... + 25.132...
= 100.530... = **100.5 cm² (1 d.p.)**

The surface area of a solid is equal to the area of its net...

You have to be a bit careful when finding the surface area of a triangular prism — the rectangles will be different sizes (unless the triangle is equilateral), so don't get caught out.

1) Draw the net of a pentagon-based pyramid.

2) What is the surface area of the regular tetrahedron shown, given that area A = 3 cm²?

Volume

Now it's time to work out the volumes of 3D shapes.

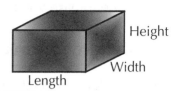
Height
Width
Length

Volumes of Cuboids

A <u>cuboid</u> is a <u>rectangular block</u>. Finding its volume is dead easy:

| Volume of a Cuboid = length × width × height | $V = l \times w \times h$ |

You can count the number of cubes in a shape to find the volume, or use the formula above.

Example

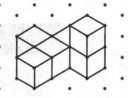

In the diagram, each cube has a volume of 1 cm³. What is the volume of the whole shape?

1) Count the number of cubes.   **6 cubes**

2) Multiply the number of cubes   **6 × 1 cm³ = 6 cm³**
   by the volume of each cube.

Find the volume of a cuboid with a length of 5 cm, a width of 7 cm and a height of 9 cm.

Use the <u>formula</u> $V = l \times w \times h$
for volume and $= 5 \times 7 \times 9$
plug in the values. $= 315$ **cm³**

Don't forget your units — it'll always be 'something-cubed'.

Volumes of Prisms and Cylinders

<u>A PRISM</u> is a solid (3D) object which is the same shape all the way through — i.e. it has a <u>CONSTANT AREA OF CROSS-SECTION</u>.

Triangular Prism

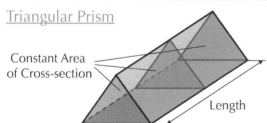
Constant Area of Cross-section
Length

Volume of Prism = cross-sectional area × length

$$V = A \times L$$

Prisms are sometimes called 'right prisms'.

Cylinder

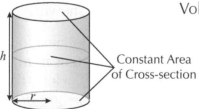
h
Constant Area of Cross-section
r

Volume of Cylinder = area of circle × height

$$V = \pi r^2 h$$

Cylinders are sometimes called 'right cylinders'.

Example

Rufus has a cylindrical jar of jam with radius 3 cm and height 10 cm. What is the volume of the jar to 3 s.f.?

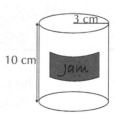
3 cm
10 cm
jam

Just put the measurements into the <u>formula</u> above:

$V = \pi r^2 h = \pi \times 3^2 \times 10 = 282.743... $ cm³ $= 283$ cm³ (3 s.f.)

Master the formulas above and you've mastered volume...

1) The cross-sectional area of an octagonal prism is 28 cm².
   The length of the prism is 6 cm. Find the volume of the prism.

Angle Basics

Here's a page to ease you into the world of all things angles.

Fancy **Angle Names**

Some angles have special names that you need to know.

Acute angles

Sharp pointy ones
(less than 90°)

Right angles

Square corners
(exactly 90°)

Obtuse angles

Flatter ones
(between 90° and 180°)

Reflex angles

Ones that bend
back on themselves
(more than 180°)

Three-Letter Angle Notation

The best way to say which angle you're talking about in a diagram is by using THREE letters. For example in the diagram, angle BAC = 35°.

1) The middle letter is where the angle is.
2) The other two letters tell you which two lines enclose the angle.

NOT TO SCALE

angle ACD = 20°

You might see angles written in other ways as well — ∠ABC and AB̂C are both the same as angle ABC.

Drawing Angles with a **Protractor**

Draw a straight horizontal line to be your base line. Put the protractor on the line so that the middle of the protractor is on one end of the line as shown:

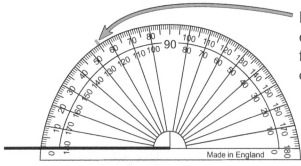

Draw a little line or dot next to the angle you're drawing (count up in tens from 0° to make sure you follow the right scale). Here, I'm drawing an angle of 55°, so I'm using the outside scale.

Be careful — reading from the wrong scale is a very very common error.

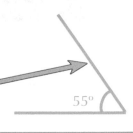

Then join your base line to the mark you've just made with a straight line. You must join the end of the base line that was in the middle of the protractor.

55°

If my cat were an angle, she'd be acute one...

Make sure you learn all the different angle names, and know how to use your protractor.

1) Write down the names of the following angles: a) 98°   b) 234°   c) 11°

Geometry Rules

The angle rules on this page are really important — so make sure you learn them all.

6 Simple Rules — that's all

1) Angles in a **triangle** add up to **180°**.

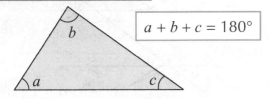

$a + b + c = 180°$

2) Angles on a **straight line** add up to **180°**.

$a + b + c = 180°$

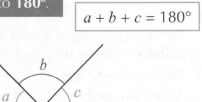

3) Angles in a **quadrilateral** add up to **360°**.

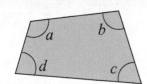

Remember that a quadrilateral is a 4-sided shape.

$a + b + c + d = 360°$

4) Angles round a **point** add up to **360°**.

$a + b + c + d = 360°$

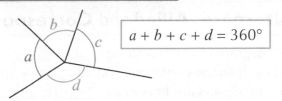

5) Exterior angle of a triangle = sum of opposite interior angles.

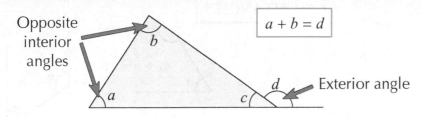

$a + b = d$

Opposite interior angles

Exterior angle

6) Isosceles triangles have **2 sides** the same and **2 angles** the same.

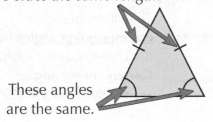

These dashes indicate two sides the same length.

These angles are the same.

Example

Find the size of angle _x_.

The two angles at the bottom are <u>the same</u> (they're both 75°), so
75° + 75° + _x_ = 180°
_x_ = 180° − 150°
_x_ = 30°

In an isosceles triangle, you only need to know one angle to be able to find the other two.

No excuses for not learning these six simple rules...

None of the rules here are particularly difficult, but make sure you don't get them mixed up. Once you're happy with them all, have a go at this question.

1) Find the size of angle _x_ in the diagram on the right.

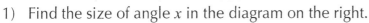
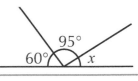

Intersecting and Parallel Lines

Parallel lines are always the same distance apart (and never meet).
Perpendicular lines are always at right angles to each other (they meet at 90°).

Perpendicular lines

Angles Around **Parallel Lines**

When a line <u>intersects</u> two <u>parallel lines</u>,
it forms special sets of angles.

1) The two <u>bunches</u> of angles formed at the
points of intersection <u>are the same</u>.

2) There are only actually <u>two different angles</u> involved
(labelled *a* and *b* here), and they add up to <u>180°</u>
(from rule 2 on page 93).

3) <u>Vertically opposite angles</u> (ones opposite each other) are <u>equal</u>
(in the diagram, *a* and *a* are vertically opposite, as are *b* and *b*).

These arrows show that
the lines are <u>parallel</u>.

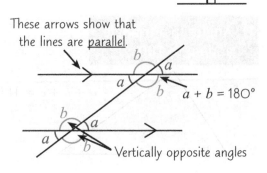

a + *b* = 180°

Vertically opposite angles

Alternate, Allied and **Corresponding** Angles

The diagram above has some <u>characteristic shapes</u> to look out for —
and each shape contains a specific <u>pair of angles</u>.
The angle pairs are known as <u>alternate</u>, <u>allied</u> and <u>corresponding angles</u>.

You need to spot the <u>characteristic Z, C, U and F shapes</u>:

ALTERNATE ANGLES

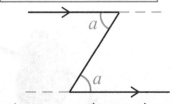

<u>Alternate</u> angles are the <u>same</u>.
They are found in a <u>Z-shape</u>.

ALLIED ANGLES

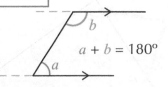

a + *b* = 180°

<u>Allied</u> angles <u>add up to 180°</u>.
They are found in a <u>C- or U-shape</u>.

CORRESPONDING ANGLES

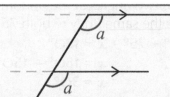

<u>Corresponding</u> angles are the <u>same</u>.
They are found in an <u>F-shape</u>.

Example

Find the size of angle *x*.

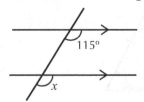

115°

x

This diagram shows
<u>corresponding angles</u> (spot
the characteristic F-shape).
Corresponding angles
are the same, so ***x* = 115°**

Keep your eyes peeled for the Z, C, U and F shapes...

It's OK to use the letters Z, C, U and F to help you identify the angles,
but make sure you know the proper names too.

1) Find the size of angle *y* in the diagram on the right.

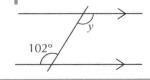

y

102°

Geometry Problems

Now it's time to put your knowledge to use, and solve some geometry problems.

Try Out All the Rules One by One

1) If you're stuck, don't concentrate too much on the angle you have been asked to find. Find ALL the angles in whatever order they become obvious.

2) Don't sit there waiting for inspiration to hit you. It's all too easy to find yourself staring at a geometry problem and getting nowhere. The method is this:

GO THROUGH ALL THE RULES OF GEOMETRY (including PARALLEL LINES), ONE BY ONE, and apply each of them in turn in as many ways as possible — one of them is bound to work.

Example

Find the size of angle x.

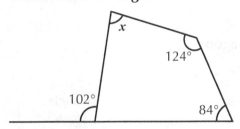

Angles on a straight line add up to 180°. So the missing angle in the quadrilateral is
180° − 102° = 78°

Angles in a quadrilateral add up to 360°, so
x + 78° + 124° + 84° = 360°
x = 360° − 78° − 124° − 84° = **74°**

Example

Find the size of angle x. Give a reason for each step of your working.

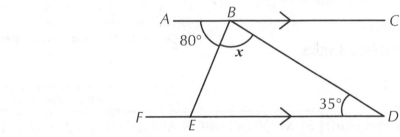

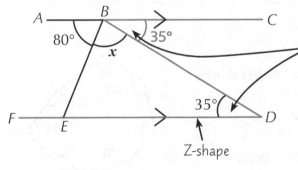

1) Notice that AC and FD are parallel.
CBD and BDE are alternate angles.
So CBD = 35°

2) Now you know two angles on straight line AC.
Angles on a straight line add up to 180°.
So x = 180° − 80° − 35°
= **65°**

If at first you don't succeed, try the next rule of geometry...

1) Find the size of angle BEF in the diagram above.

Exterior and Interior Angles

You're not quite done with angles yet (sorry) — now it's time for angles in polygons.

Exterior and Interior Angles

You need to know <u>what</u> exterior and interior angles in polygons are and <u>how to find them</u>.

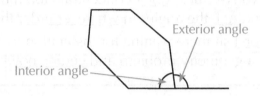

For <u>ANY POLYGON</u> (regular or irregular):

SUM OF EXTERIOR ANGLES = 360°

INTERIOR ANGLE = 180° – EXTERIOR ANGLE

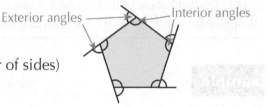

For <u>REGULAR POLYGONS</u>:

EXTERIOR ANGLE = $\dfrac{360°}{n}$ (*n* is the number of sides)

Example

Find the exterior and interior angles of a regular hexagon.

Hexagons have 6 sides: exterior angle = $\dfrac{360°}{n}$ = $\dfrac{360°}{6}$ = **60°**

Use the exterior angle to find the interior angle: interior angle = 180° – exterior angle

= 180° – 60° = **120°**

Example

What regular polygon has exterior angles of 72°?

1) Put 72° into the formula 'exterior angle = $\dfrac{360°}{n}$' $72° = \dfrac{360°}{n}$

2) Rearrange the equation and do the division to work out the <u>number of sides</u>. $n = \dfrac{360°}{72°}$ = 5, so it's a regular **pentagon**

Sum of Interior Angles

n is the number of sides

For <u>ANY POLYGON</u> (regular or irregular):   SUM OF INTERIOR ANGLES = $(n - 2) \times 180°$

Example

Find the value of *x* in the diagram on the right.

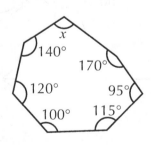

1) First, find the <u>sum of the interior angles</u> of the 7-sided shape:
   Sum of interior angles = $(n - 2) \times 180°$
   = $(7 - 2) \times 180°$ = 900°

2) Now write an <u>equation</u> and <u>solve it</u> to find *x*:
   x + 170° + 95° + 115° + 100° + 120° + 140° = 900°
   x = 900° – 170° – 95° – 115° – 100° – 120° – 140° = **160°**

Exterior angles of any polygon always add up to 360°...

1) Work out the size of an exterior angle and an interior angle of a regular octagon.

Transformations

The next few pages are all about transformations — translation, reflection, rotation, enlargement.

1) Translations

A translation is just a <u>SLIDE</u> around the page. When describing a translation, you must say <u>how far right or left</u> and <u>how far up or down</u> the shape moves.

Example

Translate square A 3 units right and 2 units up. Label it 'B'.

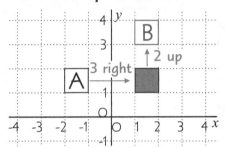

Follow the instructions:

1) Move the square <u>3 places</u> to the <u>right</u>...

2) ...and then <u>2 places up</u>.

Describe the transformation that maps:

a) **Triangle A onto triangle B.**

A translation of 5 units left and 6 units down.

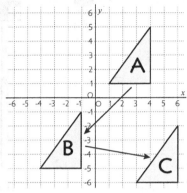

b) **Triangle B onto triangle C.**

A translation of 7 units right and 1 unit down.

2) Reflections

⎰⎰⎰ See p.51 for more on straight lines. ⎰⎰⎰

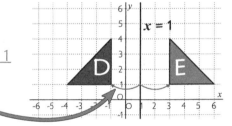

Triangle D is mapped onto triangle E by a <u>reflection</u> in the line $x = 1$
Notice that the matching corners are <u>equal distances</u> from the mirror line.
To describe a <u>reflection</u>, you must give the <u>equation</u> of the <u>mirror line</u>.

Example

Describe the transformation that maps:

a) **Shape F onto shape G.**
   A reflection in the x-axis

b) **Shape G onto shape H.**
   A reflection in the line $y = x$

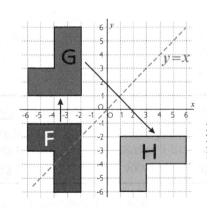

⎰⎰⎰ Any shape that is a translation, reflection or rotation is congruent to the original shape (see p.100). ⎰⎰⎰

My favourite kind of transformation occurs every full moon...

Remember what information you have to give for each transformation — for a translation, you need to give instructions, and for a reflection, you need to give the equation of the mirror line.

1) Describe the transformation that maps triangle A onto triangle C in the diagram above.

Transformations

Transformation number 3 coming up — rotation.

3) Rotations

To describe a rotation, you need 3 details:

1) The angle of rotation (usually 90° or 180°).
2) The direction of rotation (clockwise or anticlockwise).
3) The centre of rotation

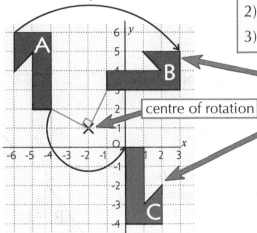

centre of rotation

Shape A is mapped onto Shape B by a rotation of 90° clockwise about point (–2, 1).

Shape A is mapped onto Shape C by a rotation of 180° about point (–2, 1).

For a rotation of 180°, it doesn't matter whether you go clockwise or anticlockwise.

You could be asked about quarter turns or half turns — a quarter turn is just a 90° turn, and a half turn is just a 180° turn. Easy.

Example

Rotate Triangle D a quarter turn clockwise about (0, 0).

The best way to tackle this is with tracing paper:

1) Trace the shape and mark the centre of rotation at (0, 0).
2) Put your pencil point on the centre of rotation and rotate the tracing paper a quarter turn clockwise — that's 90° clockwise. You'll know when you've gone far enough — the horizontal side will be vertical, and vice versa.
3) Mark the corners of the shape in their new positions on the grid, then draw the shape.

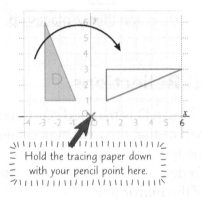

Hold the tracing paper down with your pencil point here.

Example

Describe the transformation that maps Triangle E onto Triangle F.

A half turn, or a rotation of 180°, about (–1, O).

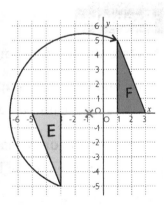

You can use tracing paper to help you find the centre of rotation. Trace the original shape and then try putting your pencil on different points until the traced shape rotates onto the image. When this happens your pencil must be on the centre of rotation.

Rotations — they're a real page-turner...

1) Square S has side length 1 unit and its bottom-left corner is at the coordinates (2, 3).
   a) Draw square S.   b) Rotate square S 180° about (0, 1) and label it T.
2) Triangle G has corners (–3, 2), (–3, 4) and (–8, 2). Draw triangles F (above) and G on a graph, and describe the rotation that maps triangle F onto triangle G.

Transformations

You've made it to the final transformation now — get ready for enlargements.

4) Enlargements

The scale factor for an enlargement tells you <u>how long</u> the sides of the new shape are compared to the old shape. E.g. a scale factor of 3 means you <u>multiply</u> each side length by 3.
The <u>centre of enlargement</u> tells you where to start your enlargement from.

Example

Enlarge shape X by a scale factor of 2 with centre of enlargement C.

Start by finding where one corner will go — <u>draw a line</u> from C
to the bottom-left of X, and then draw the same length <u>again</u>.
Do the same for <u>every</u> corner and <u>join up</u> the points.
Each side will be <u>twice as long</u> as the matching side on shape X.

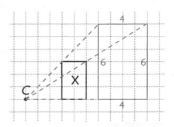

The <u>area</u> of an enlarged shape has the area of the <u>original shape</u> multiplied by the scale factor <u>squared</u>.

Example

The area of a triangle is 5 cm². It is then enlarged by a scale factor of 3.
What is the area of the enlarged triangle?

Multiply the <u>original area</u> by the <u>scale factor squared</u>. $5 \times 3^2 = 5 \times 9 = 45$ cm²

Describing an Enlargement

To DESCRIBE an <u>ENLARGEMENT</u>, you need:

1) The <u>scale factor</u>.
2) The <u>centre of enlargement</u>.

$$\text{scale factor} = \frac{\text{new length}}{\text{old length}}$$

Example

Describe the transformation that maps Triangle A onto Triangle B.

Use the formula to find the <u>scale factor</u>. (Just do this for one pair of sides.)

Old length of triangle base = 2 units
New length of triangle base = 4 units

$$\text{scale factor} = \frac{\text{new length}}{\text{old length}} = \frac{4}{2} = 2$$

Enlargements give
similar shapes —
see p.101.

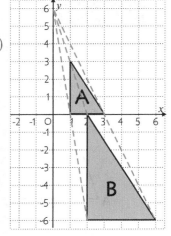

To find the <u>centre of enlargement</u>, draw <u>lines</u> that go through <u>matching corners</u> of both shapes and see where they <u>cross</u>.

So the transformation is an enlargement of scale factor 2, centre (0, 6).

An enlargement changes the size of a shape...

1) Plot the triangles X (1, 2), (–1, 3), (–1, 5) and Y (7, –4), (1, –1), (1, 5)
   and work out the scale factor for the transformation that maps triangle X onto triangle Y.

Congruent Shapes

Congruence is another word which sounds really complicated when it's not.
If two shapes are congruent, they are the same size and have the same shape.

CONGRUENT

A   B

same size, same shape

Showing Triangles are Congruent

To prove that <u>two triangles</u> are <u>congruent</u>, you have
to show that <u>one</u> of the conditions below is true:

1) <u>SSS</u>   <u>three sides</u> are the same
2) <u>AAS</u>   <u>two angles</u> and a <u>corresponding side</u> match up
3) <u>SAS</u>   <u>two sides</u> and the <u>angle between them</u> match up
4) <u>RHS</u>   a <u>right angle</u>, the <u>hypotenuse</u> and one other <u>side</u> all match up

The hypotenuse is the longest side of a right-angled triangle — the one opposite the right angle.

Make sure the sides match up — here, the side is opposite the 81° angle.

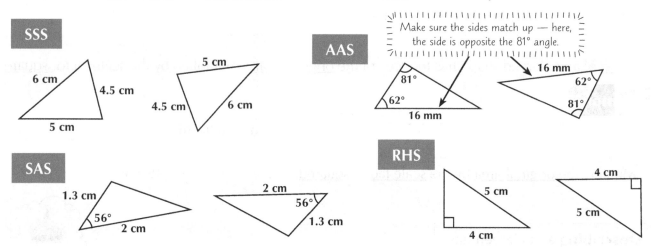

Work Out All the Sides and Angles You Can Find

The best approach to proving two triangles are congruent is to <u>write down everything</u>
you can find out, then see which <u>condition</u> they fit.

Example

Show that the triangles ABD and CBD below are congruent.

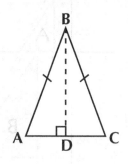

<u>Write down</u> what you know:

- Both triangles have a <u>right angle</u> (ADB and CDB)
  as angles on a straight line add up to 180°.

- AB and CB are the same length (as it's an isosceles triangle)
  — these sides are the <u>hypotenuse</u> of each triangle.

- BD is a side in both triangles, so it's the <u>same length</u>.

The condition <u>RHS</u> holds, so ABD and CBD are congruent triangles.

Congruent shapes are like two peas in a pod...

1) Are the two triangles on the right
   congruent? Explain your answer.

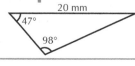

Similar Shapes

Similar shapes are exactly the same shape but different sizes (they can also be rotated or reflected).

Similar Shapes Have the Same Angles

Two shapes are <u>similar</u> if:

1) All the <u>angles</u> match up.
2) The <u>sides</u> are all enlarged by the <u>same scale factor</u>.

Each side in the larger triangle is twice as long as in the smaller triangle.

<u>Angles</u> match up in <u>both triangles</u>:

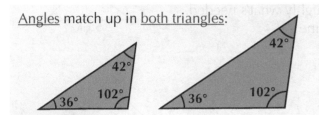

Each <u>side</u> is <u>enlarged</u> by the <u>same scale factor</u>:

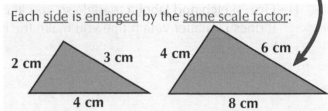

Example

Shape B is similar to shape A. Find the scale factor of enlargement from A to B.

This question is tricky because the shapes aren't the same way up. Make sure you're comparing <u>matching sides</u>.

Longest side of B = 4 units
Longest side of A = 2 units

$$\text{scale factor} = \frac{\text{new length}}{\text{old length}} = \frac{4}{2} = 2$$

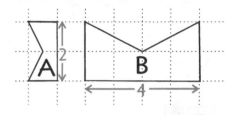

Use the Scale Factor to Find Missing Sides

Exam questions often ask you to find the <u>length</u> of a <u>missing side</u> or the <u>size</u> of a <u>missing angle</u> in a pair of similar shapes.

Example

Shapes ABCDE and FGHJK are similar. The scale factor of enlargement from ABCDE to FGHJK is 4.

a) **Write down the value of x.**

The shapes are <u>similar</u> so the angles <u>match up</u>. The angle at C corresponds with the angle at H, so they both must be 106°.

$$x = 106°$$

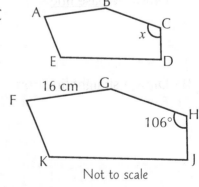

b) **Calculate the length of side AB.**

The scale factor is 4 so each side in FGHJK must be <u>4 times as big</u> as the corresponding side in ABCDE. FG corresponds with AB.

Length of AB = Length of FG ÷ 4
= 16 cm ÷ 4 = **4 cm**

Similar shapes are the same shape, but a different size...

1) The scale factor of enlargement between two similar triangles is 3. The longest side of the larger triangle is 18 cm. How long is the longest side of the smaller triangle?

Section 5 — Geometry and Measures

Triangle Construction

How you construct a triangle depends on what information you're given about the triangle...

Sides Only — Use a **Ruler and Compasses**

Example

Construct the triangle *ABC* where *AB* = 5 cm, *BC* = 3 cm, *AC* = 4 cm.

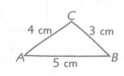

1) First, <u>sketch and label</u> a triangle so you know roughly what's needed. It doesn't matter which line you make the base line.

 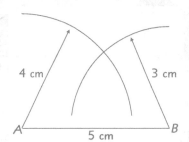 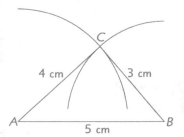

2) Draw the <u>base line</u>. Label the ends *A* and *B*.

3) For *AC*, set the <u>compasses</u> to <u>4 cm</u>, put the point at *A* and <u>draw an arc</u>. For *BC*, set the compasses to <u>3 cm</u>, put the point at *B* and <u>draw an arc</u>.

4) Where the <u>arcs cross</u> is <u>point C</u>. Now you can finish your triangle.

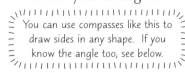
You can use compasses like this to draw sides in any shape. If you know the angle too, see below.

Sides and **Angles** — Use a **Ruler** and **Protractor**

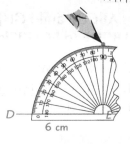
You could also use a set square to draw a right angle.

Example

Construct triangle *DEF*. *DE* = 6 cm, *DEF* = 90°, and angle *EDF* = 40°.

1) <u>Roughly sketch and label</u> the triangle.

2) Draw the <u>base line</u>.

3) Draw <u>angle *DEF*</u> (the angle at *E*) — place the centre of the protractor over *E*, measure <u>90°</u> and put a dot.

4) Draw a <u>straight line</u> from *E* going through the dot.

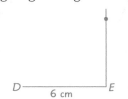

5) Do steps 3 and 4 again, but this time for <u>angle *EDF*</u>.

6) <u>Label</u> the point where the two lines meet <u>*F*</u>.

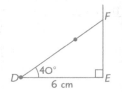

Always sketch the triangle out first...

1) Construct a triangle with sides 3 cm, 4 cm and 4 cm. Leave your construction marks showing.

Pythagoras' Theorem

Pythagoras' theorem sounds scary but it's actually OK. There's just one little formula to learn...

Pythagoras' Theorem — $a^2 + b^2 = c^2$

1) PYTHAGORAS' THEOREM only works for RIGHT-ANGLED TRIANGLES.
2) Pythagoras uses two sides to find the third side.
3) The BASIC FORMULA for Pythagoras is $a^2 + b^2 = c^2$.
4) Make sure you get the numbers in the RIGHT PLACE. c is the longest side (called the hypotenuse) and it's always opposite the right angle.
5) Always CHECK that your answer is SENSIBLE.

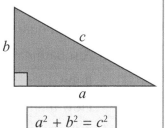

$$a^2 + b^2 = c^2$$

Example

Find the length of SU to 3 significant figures.
Put the numbers into the formula
(notice that ST is the hypotenuse):

$SU^2 + 5^2 = 11^2$

$SU^2 + 25 = 121$

$\quad SU^2 = 121 - 25 = 96$

$\quad SU = \sqrt{96} = 9.797... = 9.80$ m (to 3 s.f.)

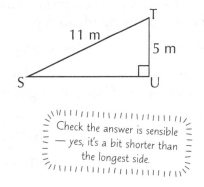

Check the answer is sensible — yes, it's a bit shorter than the longest side.

Example

Find the distance between points S and T to 1 d.p.

1) Work out the coordinates of S and T. $\quad S = (1, 2) \qquad T = (6, 5)$

2) Work out the horizontal distance between S and T. $\quad$ Horizontal = $6 - 1 = 5$ units

3) Now find the vertical distance between S and T. $\quad$ Vertical = $5 - 2 = 3$ units

4) The distance between S and T is the hypotenuse (c) of the triangle. So substitute these values into the equation for Pythagoras' theorem.

$\quad 5^2 + 3^2 = c^2$

$\quad 34 = c^2$

$\quad c = \sqrt{34}$

$\quad c = 5.8309... = 5.8$ units (to 1 d.p.)

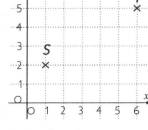

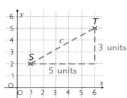

If you're getting a bit confused, here's a quick summary of what you have to do:

1) **SQUARE THEM** — SQUARE THE TWO NUMBERS that you are given, (use the x^2 button if you've got your calculator).

2) **ADD or SUBTRACT** — To find the longest side, ADD the two squared numbers. To find a shorter side, SUBTRACT the smaller one from the larger.

3) **SQUARE ROOT** — Finally, take the SQUARE ROOT (use the $\sqrt{}$ button on your calculator).

Pythagoras' theorem is as easy as a, b, c...

1) The two shorter sides of a right-angled triangle are 5 cm and 12 cm long. Find the longest side.

Warm-Up and Practice Questions

We meet again — have a go at the questions below to see how much you know about geometry.

Warm-Up Questions

1) Which quadrilateral has no lines of symmetry but rotational symmetry of order 2?

2) A square has a perimeter of 24 cm. Find its area.

3) If the diameter of a circle is 6 cm, what is its radius?

4) How many vertices does a square-based pyramid have?

5) Find the surface area of a cylinder that has a radius of 5 cm and a height of 12 cm. Give your answer to 1 decimal place.

6) Three internal angles in a quadrilateral are 65°, 87° and 125°. What is the size of the fourth angle?

7) What type of angles do you find in an F-shape on parallel lines?

8) Triangle T has corners (2, 2), (3, 4) and (4, 2) and triangle S has corners (4, –3), (2, –2) and (2, –4). Draw triangles T and S on a graph and describe the transformation that maps T onto S.

9) The length of one side of a shape is 4 cm. When the shape is enlarged, the same side measures 12 cm. What is the scale factor of the enlargement?

10) A triangle has sides of length 8 cm, 15 cm and 17 cm. Use Pythagoras' theorem to check whether it is a right-angled triangle.

Practice Questions

1) a) Draw the lines of symmetry on this square.

You should know that a square has 4 lines of symmetry. That way you won't forget any.

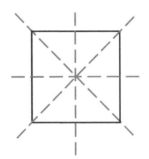

Remember, a line of symmetry is a line along which the two halves of a shape will fold exactly together.

[2 marks]

b) Add a ☐ to make this shape symmetrical. Find the 3 different ways to do it.

(i) 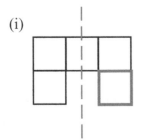   (ii) 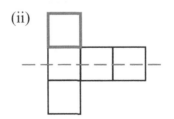   (iii)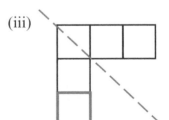

[3 marks]

Check what you've done by adding the line of symmetry. You should be able to see whether your new shape will fold exactly together along it.

Practice Questions

2) Find the area of the shaded region in the diagram below. Give your answer to 1 decimal place.

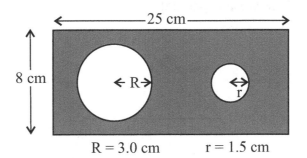

(not to scale)

R = 3.0 cm   r = 1.5 cm

....
[4 marks]

3) Look at the cuboid and net below.

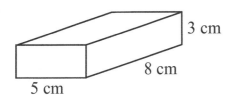

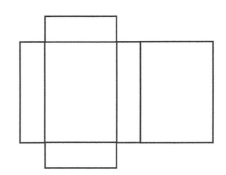

Use the net to find the total surface area.

....
[3 marks]

4) The diagram shows part of a regular polygon.

(not to scale)

150°

How many sides does it have?

....
[2 marks]

Practice Questions

5) In the diagram, which is not drawn to scale, the straight lines ABG and DEF are parallel.
The straight lines BEC and GF are also parallel.

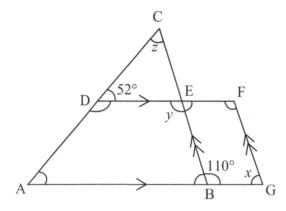

Find the size of angles x, y, z.

$x =$ ....

$y =$ ....

$z =$ ....

[4 marks]

6) Look at the four trapeziums drawn on this coordinate grid.

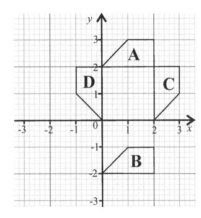

a) Describe completely the transformation that maps A to C.

....

....

[2 marks]

b) Describe completely the transformation that maps D onto B.

....

....

[3 marks]

Practice Questions

7) Find the volume of the cylinder below, to 1 decimal place.

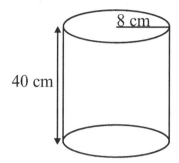

[4 marks]

8) Quadrilateral B is an enlargement of quadrilateral A.

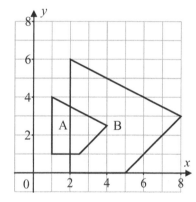

Describe the transformation that maps quadrilateral A onto quadrilateral B.

....

....

[3 marks]

9) An equilateral triangle has sides of length 4 cm. Find its height to 1 decimal place.

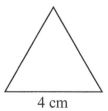

4 cm

....

[3 marks]

Summary Questions

Congratulations — you've got to the end. Section 5 is a tough one so here's some practice for you.
- Try these questions and <u>tick off each one</u> when you <u>get it right</u>.
- When you've done <u>all the questions</u> for a topic and are <u>completely happy</u>, tick off the topic.

<u>2D Shapes (p.81-83)</u> ☐

1) Write down the number of lines of symmetry
   and the order of rotational symmetry for a rhombus. ☐
2) Name 2 quadrilaterals that have 2 pairs of equal angles. ☐
3) A regular polygon has 8 sides. What is the name of this polygon? ☐

<u>Perimeter and Area (p.84-87)</u> ☐

4) Find the perimeter and area of a rectangle that measures 11 cm by 5 cm. ☐
5) A rectangle has a perimeter of 68 cm.
   If one of its sides is 4 cm long, what is its area? ☐
6) Find the area of the shape on the right. ☐
7) Find the area of a circle with radius 8 cm, to 2 decimal places. ☐
8) Find the area of a sector with an internal angle of 72° in
   a circle with radius 6 cm to 1 decimal place. ☐

7 cm
4 cm
4 cm

<u>3D Shapes (p.88-91)</u> ☐

9) Write down the number of faces and edges of a cube. ☐
10) Draw the net of a cuboid measuring 2 cm by 3 cm by 5 cm.
    Find the cuboid's volume and surface area. ☐
11) Find the volume of a prism with cross-sectional area 6 cm² and length 8 cm. ☐

<u>Angles (p.92-96)</u> ☐

12) Give an example of a) an acute angle, b) an obtuse angle, c) a reflex angle. ☐
13) What type of angles do you find in a Z-shape on parallel lines? ☐
14) Find the size of angle x in the diagram on the right. ☐
15) Work out the size of an exterior angle and an interior angle
    of a regular decagon (a 10-sided shape). ☐

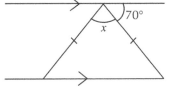

70°
x

<u>Transformations, Congruence and Similarity (p.97-101)</u> ☐

16) Point P (3, 4) is reflected in the line $y = 2$. What are the new coordinates of point P? ☐
17) A triangle has vertices with coordinates (1, 1), (4, 1) and (3, 4). Write the coordinates
    of the vertices of the triangle after an enlargement with scale factor 3 and centre (–1, 0). ☐
18) Write down the 4 different conditions you can use to show that triangles are congruent. ☐
19) Write down the two properties that similar shapes have. ☐

<u>Triangle Construction and Pythagoras' Theorem (p.102-103)</u> ☐

20) Construct triangle ABC, where $AB = 3$ cm, $AC = 3.5$ cm and angle $CAB = 50°$. ☐
21) Use Pythagoras' theorem to find the length of the missing side to 3 s.f. ☐
22) Find the distance between the coordinates (–1, 2) and (2, 6). ☐

10 cm
7 cm

Probability

Believe me, probability's not as bad as you think it is, but you must learn the basic facts.

All Probabilities are Between 0 and 1

Probabilities can only have values <u>from 0 to 1</u> (including those values).
You can show the probability of any event happening on this <u>scale</u> of 0 to 1.

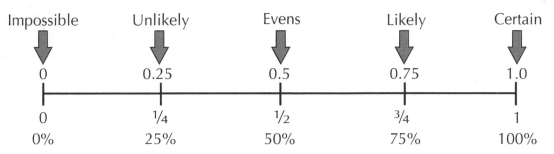

Impossible	Unlikely	Evens	Likely	Certain
0	0.25	0.5	0.75	1.0
0	¼	½	¾	1
0%	25%	50%	75%	100%

If All the Outcomes are Equally Likely, Use This Formula

<u>Outcomes</u> are just 'things that could happen'. If you repeat an experiment, you can get <u>different</u> outcomes — think, if you keep rolling a fair dice, you're likely to get different numbers.

Use the formula below to find probabilities for a <u>fair</u> spinner, coin or dice.
A spinner/coin/dice is 'fair' when it's <u>equally likely</u> to land on <u>any</u> of its sides.

$$\text{Probability} = \frac{\text{Number of ways for something to happen}}{\text{Total number of possible outcomes}}$$

This formula works for other cases where all the possible outcomes are <u>equally likely</u> (so in the example below, there's an <u>equal chance</u> of picking any one ball).

Example

A bag contains 6 blue balls, 6 red balls and 9 green balls.
Find the probability of picking out a green ball.

Just put the numbers into the formula above:

P(green) means 'the probability of picking green'.

$$P(\text{green}) = \frac{\text{Number of green balls}}{\text{Total number of balls}} = \frac{9}{21} = \frac{3}{7}$$

Always give fractions in their simplest form.

Probabilities Add Up to 1

1) If <u>only one</u> possible result can happen at a time, then the probabilities of <u>all</u> the results <u>add up to 1</u>.

2) So since something must either <u>happen</u> or <u>not happen</u> (i.e. <u>only one</u> of these can happen at a time):

3) In the example above, the probability of <u>not</u> picking green = 1 – P(green) = 1 – 0.45 = <u>0.55</u>.

> Probabilities always ADD UP to 1
>
> P(event happens) + P(event doesn't happen) = 1

A probability close to 1 means an event is likely to happen...

1) On a fair 10-sided spinner numbered 1-10, what is the probability of spinning:
   a) 7?   b) An odd number?   c) An even number?

 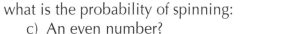

Probability

Probability gets more interesting when more than one thing is happening at the same time.

Use Tables to List All Possible Outcomes

When there are <u>multiple things</u> happening you can use a <u>table</u> to list all the possible outcomes.

Example

The two fair spinners on the right are each spun once.

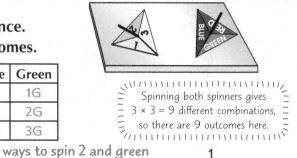

a) **Complete this table showing the possible outcomes.**

The possible outcomes for one spinner go <u>down the side</u>. The outcomes for the other spinner go <u>along the top</u>.

	Red	Blue	Green
1	1R	1B	1G
2	2R	2B	2G
3	3R	3B	3G

Spinning both spinners gives 3 × 3 = 9 different combinations, so there are 9 outcomes here.

b) **Find the probability of spinning a 2 and a green (2G).**

$$P(2G) = \frac{\text{ways to spin 2 and green}}{\text{total number of possible outcomes}} = \frac{1}{9}$$

c) **Find the probability of spinning an odd number and a red.**

1R and 3R

$$P(\text{odd and red}) = \frac{\text{ways to spin odd and red}}{\text{total number of possible outcomes}} = \frac{2}{9}$$

Example

A coin is tossed three times. Find the probability of getting heads exactly twice.

There are 3 ways to get heads <u>exactly twice</u>: (HHT), (HTH) and (THH), and <u>8 possible outcomes</u> in total.

$$P(\text{two heads}) = \frac{\text{ways to throw heads twice}}{\text{total number of possible outcomes}} = \frac{3}{8}$$

	Possible Outcomes							
Throw 1	H	H	H	T	H	T	T	T
Throw 2	H	H	T	H	T	H	T	T
Throw 3	H	T	H	H	T	T	H	T

Use Probability to Find an "Expected Frequency"

1) Once you know the <u>probability</u> of something, you can <u>predict</u> how many times it will happen in a certain number of trials.

2) For example, if you tossed a fair coin 50 times, you would expect to get about 25 heads. This prediction is called the <u>expected frequency</u>.

$$\boxed{\text{Expected frequency} = \text{probability} \times \text{number of trials}}$$

Example

The probability of someone winning a game at a fair is 0.12. Estimate the number of times you would expect them to win if they played the game 50 times.

Expected number of wins = probability of a win × number of trials

$$= 0.12 \times 50 = 6$$

This is an estimate. They might not win exactly 6 times, but it should be close.

The expected frequency is only an estimate...

1) Two fair dice numbered 1-6 are rolled, and their scores added together. By listing all the possible outcomes in a table, find the probability that the total score is greater than 7.

2) A spinner has a probability of 0.3 of landing on blue. If the spinner is spun 40 times, estimate how many times you would expect it to land on blue.

Experimental Probability

Dice aren't always fair — you can use experimental probability to decide if they are or aren't.

Fair or Unfair?

1) You can use the formula on p.109 to work out that the probability of rolling a 3 on a dice is $\frac{1}{6}$.
2) BUT this only works if it's a <u>fair dice</u>. If the dice is <u>unfair</u> (<u>biased</u>) then each number <u>won't</u> have an equal chance of being rolled.
3) This is where <u>experimental probability</u> is useful. You can use it to <u>estimate</u> probabilities when things aren't fair.

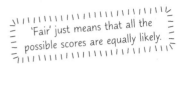
'Fair' just means that all the possible scores are equally likely.

Do the Experiment Again and Again and Again...

You need to do an experiment <u>over and over again</u> and count how often a result happens (its <u>frequency</u>). Then you can find its <u>experimental probability</u>.

$$\text{Experimental probability} = \frac{\text{Frequency}}{\text{Number of times you tried the experiment}}$$

Sometimes the experimental probability is called the 'relative frequency'.

You can use the <u>experimental probability</u> of a result as an <u>estimate</u> of its <u>probability</u>.

Example

A dice was rolled 100 times. The results are in the table on the right. Estimate the probability of getting each of the scores.

Score	1	2	3	4	5	6
Frequency	15	13	4	45	16	7

The dice was rolled <u>100 times</u>, so <u>divide</u> each of the frequencies by 100 to find the <u>experimental probabilities</u>.

Score	1	2	3	4	5	6
Experimental Probability	$\frac{15}{100}=0.15$	$\frac{13}{100}=0.13$	$\frac{4}{100}=0.04$	$\frac{45}{100}=0.45$	$\frac{16}{100}=0.16$	$\frac{7}{100}=0.07$

The <u>MORE TIMES</u> you do the experiment, the <u>MORE ACCURATE</u> your estimate of the probability will be. If you rolled the above dice <u>1000 times</u>, you'd get a <u>better</u> estimate of the probabilities.

For a <u>fair</u> dice or spinner, the experimental probabilities should all be <u>roughly the same</u> after a large number of trials. If some of them are very <u>different</u>, the dice or spinner is probably <u>biased</u>.

Example

If it's fair, you'd expect roughly the same number of each score.

Do the above results suggest that the dice is biased?
Yes, because on a <u>fair</u> dice, you'd expect all the probabilities to be about the <u>same</u> (you'd expect each probability to be about 1 ÷ 6 = 0.17(ish)). These probabilities are very <u>different</u> (the probability of rolling a 4 is <u>much higher</u> than the probability of rolling a 3), so the dice is <u>biased</u>.

I think probability is great, but maybe I'm biased...

1) A 3-sided spinner is spun 100 times — it lands on red 43 times, blue 24 times and green the other times. Calculate the experimental probability of spinning each colour.

Data and Tables

Data is what statistics is all about. You've got to collect it, process it and then interpret it.

Discrete Data Can Only Take Certain Values

1) If your data is something that's <u>countable</u> in whole numbers or can only take certain <u>individual values</u>, it's called <u>discrete data</u>. Things like the <u>number of points</u> scored in a game or the <u>number of people</u> shopping on one day are examples of discrete data.

2) Discrete data can be shown in <u>frequency tables</u> — they show <u>how many</u> things there are in each <u>category</u>.

3) You can also <u>group</u> discrete data into different <u>classes</u>. It's important that you <u>define</u> the classes well so none of them overlap — each bit of data can only go in one class.

4) Grouped data can be shown in <u>grouped frequency tables</u>. For example:

> Data that isn't discrete is called continuous.

Name	Laps	Frequency
Zac	ЖЖ ЖЖ IIII	14
Alice	ЖҜ	5

> Each tally mark represents 'one'. Tally marks are grouped into fives to make them easier to count.

Age in whole years	0 – 19	20 – 39	40 – 59	60 – 79	80 – 99
Number of people	6	13	14	8	9

Two-Way Tables Show Two Types of Information

<u>Two-way tables</u> are a kind of frequency table — they show you <u>how many</u> things are in each category, but for <u>two sets of categories</u> at once.

Example

Simon asked 40 people in his school how many musical instruments they play.
a) **Complete the two-way table to show Simon's results.**

	None	1 instrument	2 or more instruments	TOTAL	
Boys	24 – 5 – 8 = 11	8	12 – 7 = 5	24	← Total boys
Girls	7	16 – 7 – 7 = 2	7	40 – 24 = 16	← Total girls
TOTAL	11 + 7 = 18	8 + 2 = 10	12	40	← Total people

Total who don't play an instrument   Total who play 1 instrument   Total who play 2 or more instruments

To fill in a two-way table, you need to look at the <u>differences</u> between the 'TOTAL' row or column, and the other data you're given. E.g. to start you could:

- Work out the <u>number of boys</u> who play <u>2 or more instruments</u>. The <u>total number</u> of people who play <u>2 or more instruments</u> is <u>12</u>, and <u>7</u> of these are <u>girls</u>, so 12 – 7 = 5 **boys**, OR
- Work out the <u>number of girls</u> Simon asked. The <u>total number</u> of people Simon asked is <u>40</u>, and <u>24</u> of these are <u>boys</u>, so Simon asked 40 – 24 = 16 **girls**.

b) **Simon chooses someone who plays 1 instrument at random. What is the probability that it is a boy?**
1) Find the <u>total</u> number of people who play <u>1 instrument</u>.   10 people play 1 instrument
2) Find the number of these people who are <u>boys</u>.   8 boys play 1 instrument
3) Put the numbers into the <u>probability formula</u> given on page 109, and <u>simplify</u> if possible.   Probability = $\frac{8}{10} = \frac{4}{5}$

Don't be discreet about your knowledge of discrete data...

1) Look at the purple table in the example above.
   Given that a student is a girl, find the probability that she plays 1 instrument.

Sorting Information

Venn diagrams are a way of displaying data in intersecting circles — they're very pretty.

Venn Diagrams Sort Things Into Groups

Venn diagrams sort things into <u>groups</u>, where all the members of a group have a certain <u>property</u>.

E.g. All the numbers in a group are even.
   All the people in a group have brown hair.

1) Each group is represented by a <u>circle</u>. A circle can show the <u>actual members</u> of a group, or just the <u>number of members</u>.

2) There is a region where the circles <u>overlap</u>. If something fits into <u>both groups</u>, it goes here.

3) If something <u>doesn't fit</u> into a group, it goes in the <u>rectangle</u>, outside of the circles.

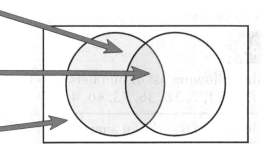

Example

A class of children were asked whether they have any brothers or sisters.
This diagram shows how many people gave each answer.

a) **How many children have only a sister?**
   This is the number in the part of the 'Sister' circle that <u>doesn't overlap</u>.   12 children

b) **How many children have a brother and a sister?**
   Children who have a brother <u>and</u> a sister are recorded in the 'overlap' region.   5 children

c) **How many children have a brother?**
   This is everyone in the 'Brother' circle, including the <u>overlap</u>.   9 + 5 = 14 children

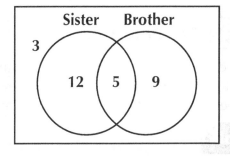

Example

Sort the following numbers into the diagram on the right:
5, 9, 11, 1, 8, 40, 12, 7, 16, 21, 24, 2, 3, 4, 44, 10

1) Start by writing out all the numbers that are <u>multiples of 4</u> and all the numbers that are <u>factors of 80</u>

   Multiples of 4 — 8, 40, 12, 16, 24, 4, 44
   Factors of 80 — 5, 1, 8, 40, 16, 2, 4, 10

2) The numbers that are in <u>both</u> lists go in the <u>overlap</u> region and the rest go in <u>just</u> 'multiples of 4' or 'factors of 80'
   Factors of 80 <u>and</u> multiples of 4 — 8, 40, 16, 4
   <u>Multiples of 4</u> — 12, 24, 44, <u>Factors of 80</u> — 5, 1, 2, 10

3) The remaining numbers go in the <u>rectangle</u>, outside the circles.
   Neither group — 9, 11, 7, 21, 3

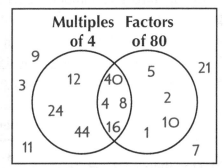

Venn diagrams don't just sort numbers — you can sort shapes, animals, people...

If in doubt, sort it out...

1) Sort the following numbers into a copy of the diagram on the right.
   9, 2, 15, 14, 11, 33, 25, 7, 12, 24, 30, 100, 73, 42, 6, 31, 28, 3, 47

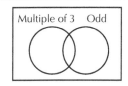

Sorting Information

Carroll diagrams are another way of sorting data visually.

Carroll Diagrams Group Things Using 'Yes' or 'No'

1) Carroll diagrams are a bit like Venn diagrams — they sort things into groups, but in table form.

2) You can sort different bits of data in a data set, according to whether they have a certain property or not. E.g. Is it less than 20 or not? Is it a factor of 60 or not? Can it fly or not?

Example

Sort the following list of numbers into the Carroll diagram below.
8, 4, 12, 6, 1, 7, 18, 36, 73, 60, 44, 54

Multiple of 6	Not a multiple of 6

18   12
  6   54
60   36
	8 44
	  1
	4 7 73

This Carroll diagram sorts numbers depending on whether they're a multiple of 6.

Go through the numbers, working out whether each one is a multiple of 6 or not. Write each number in the correct box.

Cross each number off as you go to keep track of which ones you've sorted.

Sorting By Two Properties

Carroll diagrams are often used to sort things depending on two properties.
E.g. Is it less than 7 or not AND is it an even number or not?
Does it have feathers or not AND can it fly or not?

Example

Sort the following numbers into the two diagrams below.
3, 19, 7, 20, 15, 23, 41, 55, 6, 4, 5, 14, 11, 16, 13, 37, 12, 40

Both diagrams sort numbers depending on whether they're a prime number or not, AND whether they're less than 15 or not.

1) For each number, first work out if it's a prime number or not.
2) Then work out if it's less than 15 or not.
3) Write each number in the correct part of each diagram.

Carroll and Venn diagrams are just different ways of displaying the data — they both tell you the same information.

	Prime number	Not a prime number

Less than 15	3 7 13
	  11 5
		6 4
		  14 12

Not less than 15	37 23 19 41	20 15 55 16 40

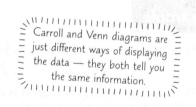

I'd put Carroll in the mathematician AND author part...

1) Draw a Carroll diagram to sort all the numbers from 1 to 15, depending on whether they're multiples of 5 or not, and whether they're factors of 20 or not.

Graphs and Charts

There are lots of diagrams for displaying data — first up is pictograms, pie charts and line graphs.

Pictograms Use Pictures Instead of Numbers

Every pictogram has a <u>key</u> telling you what one symbol represents.

With pictograms, you must use the key.

Example

This pictogram shows how many pizzas were sold by a pizzeria on different days.

a) **How many pizzas were sold on Tuesday?**
There's <u>1 whole circle</u> (= 20 pizzas)...   20 + 10
...plus <u>half</u> a circle (= 10 pizzas).   = **30 pizzas**

b) **70 pizzas were sold on Friday.**
Use this information to complete the diagram.
You need <u>3 whole circles</u> (= 60 pizzas),
<u>plus</u> another <u>half a circle</u> (= 10 pizzas). ➡

Key: ◯ represents 20 pizzas

Monday	◯ ◯
Tuesday	◯ ◖
Wednesday	◯ ◯
Thursday	◯ ◯ ◔
Friday	● ● ● ◖

Pie Charts

Learn the <u>Golden Rule</u> for pie charts: The TOTAL of Everything = 360°

Example

48 geography students were asked to name their favourite volcano.
The results are displayed in the pie chart. How many students chose Etna?
Just remember that '<u>everything = 360°</u>'.

Fraction that chose Etna = $\dfrac{\text{angle of Etna}}{\text{angle of everything}} = \dfrac{60°}{360°} = \dfrac{1}{6}$

Number of students that chose Etna = $48 \times \dfrac{1}{6} = \dfrac{48}{6} = 8$

To find the size of a sector as a percentage of the full pie chart, divide the angle by 360, then multiply by 100.

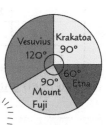

Line Graphs

1) A <u>line graph</u> is a set of points joined with straight lines.

2) They often have '<u>time</u>' along the bottom to show how something <u>changes</u> over time.

3) This graph <u>peaks</u> in <u>2011</u>, which shows that this is the year with the <u>highest sales</u>.

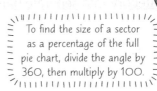

SALES OF THE BOOK: "2012: THE END OF THE WORLD"

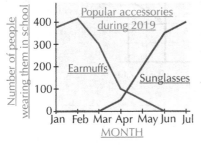

4) You can draw <u>two line graphs</u> on the same grid to <u>compare</u> two things.

5) These graphs show clearly that as the year went on, <u>fewer</u> people wore <u>earmuffs</u> and <u>more</u> people wore <u>sunglasses</u>.

Conversion graphs are another type of line graph (see page 55).

When it comes to pictograms, the key is the key...

1) In the volcano example above, how many more students chose Vesuvius than Krakatoa?

Graphs and Charts

Another page on graphs and charts — this time, it's bar charts.

Bar Charts

1) On a <u>bar chart</u>, the <u>numbers of things</u> are shown by the <u>heights</u> of the different bars.
2) <u>Bar-line graphs</u> are just like bar charts but with <u>thin lines</u> instead of bars.
3) <u>Dual bar charts</u> show two sets of data on one chart, by using <u>two bars</u> for each category.

Example

Draw a bar chart to show the data in the table below.

	Right-handed	Left-handed	Ambidextrous
Frequency	7	3	2

1) <u>Label</u> both of the <u>axes</u>.
2) <u>Draw a bar</u> for each of the <u>three categories</u>.

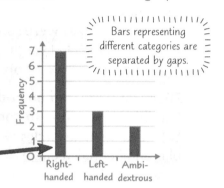

Bars representing different categories are separated by gaps.

Example

Draw a bar chart to show the data in the table below.

	Right-handed	Left-handed	Ambidextrous
Boys	3	2	1
Girls	4	1	1

Split each <u>category</u> into <u>separate bars</u> to show girls and boys.

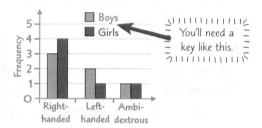

You'll need a key like this.

Frequency Bar Charts

<u>Frequency bar charts</u> are very similar to normal bar charts, but they show <u>data</u> from a <u>frequency table</u> — usually a grouped frequency table.

Example

The grouped frequency table shows the weights of 20 micro-sloths. Draw a frequency bar chart to show this information.

Weight (w kg)	Frequency
$1.0 < w \leq 1.2$	3
$1.2 < w \leq 1.4$	6
$1.4 < w \leq 1.6$	5
$1.6 < w \leq 1.8$	4
$1.8 < w \leq 2.0$	2

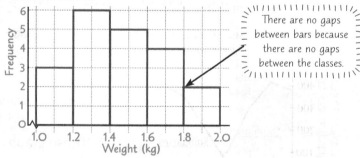

There are no gaps between bars because there are no gaps between the classes.

The taller the bar, the higher the frequency...

1) 32 pupils at a school are asked which sports team they are in. Their results are shown in the table on the right.

Use the data to draw a bar chart.

Team	Frequency
A	4
B	7
C	11
D	2
E	8

Mean, Median, Mode and Range

Mean, median, mode and range pop up all the time — make sure you know what they are.

MODE = MOST common

MEDIAN = MIDDLE value (when values are in order of size)

MEAN = TOTAL of items ÷ NUMBER of items

RANGE = Difference between highest and lowest

REMEMBER:
Mode = most (emphasise the 'mo' in each when you say them).
Median = mid (emphasise the m*d in each when you say them).
Mean is just the average, but it's mean 'cos you have to work it out.

The Golden Rule

There's one vital step for finding the median that lots of people forget:

Always REARRANGE the data in ASCENDING ORDER (and check you have the same number of entries!)

You must do this when finding the median, but it's also really useful for working out the mode.

Example

Find the median, mode, mean and range of these numbers: 6, 4, 7, 1, 2, 6, 3, 5

The MEDIAN is the middle value (when they're arranged in order of size) — so first, rearrange the numbers.

1, 2, 3, (4, 5) 6, 6, 7

Check you have the same number of values after you've rearranged them.

When there are two middle numbers, the median is halfway between the two.

← 4 numbers this side | 4 numbers this side →

Median = 4.5

MODE (or modal value) is the most common value.   Mode = 6

MEAN = $\frac{\text{total of items}}{\text{number of items}}$ $\frac{1+2+3+4+5+6+6+7}{8} = \frac{34}{8} = 4.25$

RANGE = difference between highest and lowest values, i.e. between 7 and 1: $7 - 1 = 6$

You might be asked to compare two data sets using the mean, median or mode and the range.

Example

Some children take part in a 'guess the length of the snake' competition. On the right is some information about the lengths they guess. Compare the lengths guessed by the boys and the girls.

Boys: Mean = 1.2 m
Range = 0.2 m
Girls: Mean = 2.1 m
Range = 1.4 m

1) Compare the means: The girls' mean is higher than the boys' mean, so the girls generally guessed longer lengths.

2) Compare the ranges: The girls' guesses have a bigger range, so the lengths guessed by the girls are more spread out.

Two final facts to finish: 1) Some data sets have more than one mode, or no mode at all.
2) Some measurements may be unusual, e.g. values much higher or lower than the rest. These are called outliers.

Don't mix up the different averages or you'll lose marks...

1) Find the median, mode, mean and range of these numbers: 10, 12, 8, 15, 9, 12, 11

Scatter Graphs

Scatter graphs are really useful — they show you if there's a link between two things.

Scatter Graphs Show Correlation

1) A scatter graph shows how closely two things are related.
   The fancy word for this is CORRELATION.

2) If the two things are related, then you should be able to draw a straight line
   passing pretty close to most of the points on the scatter diagram.

STRONG correlation is when your points make a fairly straight line.

WEAK correlation means your points don't line up quite so nicely (but you can still draw a line through them).

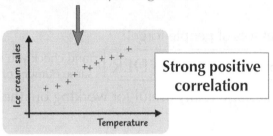

Strong positive correlation

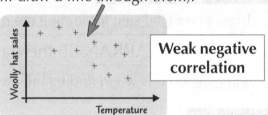

Weak negative correlation

If the points form a line sloping uphill from left to right, then there is POSITIVE correlation — both things increase or decrease together.

If the points form a line sloping downhill from left to right, then there is NEGATIVE correlation — as one quantity increases, the other decreases.

3) If the two things are not related, you get a load of messy points. This scatter graph is a messy scatter — so there's no correlation between the two things.

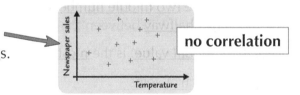

no correlation

Drawing Lines of Best Fit

A line of best fit is a straight line drawn through the middle of a set of data points.
You can use a line of best fit to predict other values.

An outlier can be ignored when drawing a line of best fit.

Example

This graph shows the value of a car (in £'000s) plotted against its age in years.

a) **Describe the strength and type of correlation shown by the graph.**
   The age of car and its value are **strongly negatively correlated**.

b) **Identify and circle the outlier on the graph.**
   The point at (5, 7.5) doesn't look like it belongs with the rest of the data, so it is an outlier.

c) **Estimate the value of a 3 year old car.**
   1) Draw a line of best fit (shown in blue).
   2) Draw a line up from 3 years to your line, and then across to the other axis.
      So a 3 year old car will be worth about **£4500**.

Outliers are any points that don't fit the overall trend...

1) Use the graph in the example above to predict the age of a car worth £3500.

 ✓ ✓ ✓

Warm-Up and Practice Questions

Hopefully the last few pages haven't been too difficult to wrap your head around. Grab your pen, put your thinking cap on and try out these questions. On your marks, get set, GO...

Warm-Up Questions

1) A random card is selected from a regular deck of playing cards. What is the probability it is:
   a) an ace?   b) a spade?   c) a multiple of 5?

2) There are 16 coloured balls in a bag. The probability of picking a red ball is P(red) = $\frac{1}{2}$.
   How many red balls are there in the bag?

3) The probability of getting green on a spinner is 0.6. If the spinner is spun 50 times, estimate how many times you would get green.

4) A pie chart is drawn, showing the favourite colours of 60 people.
   The angle for green is 72°. How many people chose green?

5) Two bar charts are drawn. One bar chart has shoe size along the horizontal axis and the other has length of feet along the horizontal axis.
   Which bar chart has gaps between the bars? Explain why this is.

6) Find the median and mean of these numbers: 8, 14, 3, 10, 4, 19, 16, 9, 7.

Practice Questions

1) Layla spins the two spinners shown below and adds the numbers to get a score.

a) Draw a diagram to show all the possible outcomes.

The 5 possible outcomes for the second spinner.

The 4 possible outcomes for the first spinner.

+	1	3	5	7	9
2	3	5	7	9	11
4	5	7	9	11	13
6	7	9	11	13	15
8	9	11	13	15	17

[3 marks]

b) Find the probability of getting a score less than 10.

There are 10 outcomes that are less than 10, out of 20 possible outcomes. → $\frac{10}{20} = \frac{1}{2}$

$\frac{1}{2}$
....
[1 mark]

c) Find the probability of getting the same number on both spinners.

The numbers on each spinner are different, so getting the same number on both spinners is impossible.

0
....
[1 mark]

Practice Questions

2) 16 students were asked how many text messages they had sent the previous day.
These were their responses:

10 18 8 3 5 15 11 3 9 8 12 32 4 9 12 9

Calculate the following:

a) the median

....
[3 marks]

b) the mode

....
[1 mark]

c) the mean

....
[3 marks]

d) the range

....
[1 mark]

e) Which of the three avaerages is the least useful for this data? Explain your answer.

....

....
[1 mark]

3) Jayan spins a four-sided spinner 20 times.
The results are recorded in the frequency table below.

Colour	Green	Blue	Red	Yellow
Frequency	5	8	1	6

a) Jayan thinks that the spinner is biased. Explain why he can't make this assumption.

....
[1 mark]

Jayan spins the spinner 80 more times. The table below shows the results for all 100 spins.

Colour	Green	Blue	Red	Yellow
Frequency	23	28	27	22

b) Do the results suggest that the spinner is biased? Explain your answer.

....

....
[2 marks]

Practice Questions

4) A group of students grew sunflowers, and measured the heights of their sunflowers after 6 weeks. Their results are recorded in the table below. Draw a frequency bar chart to show this data.

Height in m (h)	$0 \leq h < 0.5$	$0.5 \leq h < 1$	$1 \leq h < 1.5$	$1.5 \leq h < 2$	$2 \leq h < 2.5$	$2.5 \leq h < 3$
Frequency	5	12	17	20	11	10

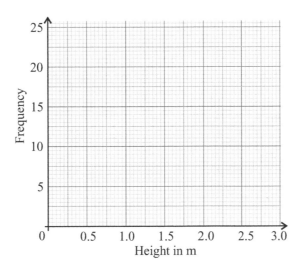

[3 marks]

5) The pie chart below shows the proportions of different sports played by 216 members of a leisure club.

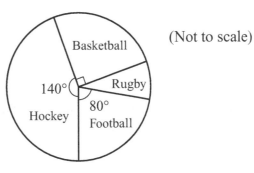

(Not to scale)

How many people at the leisure club play rugby?

....

[3 marks]

Practice Questions

6) The table shows the marks for ten pupils in their Maths and French examinations.

Pupil	Lucy	Emily	Aanya	Ismail	Nigel	Steph	Rose	Luc	Adam	Samira
Maths	45	21	39	48	26	38	45	26	8	29
French	48	28	32	44	33	40	40	28	45	34

a) Plot the data on the scatter graph below.

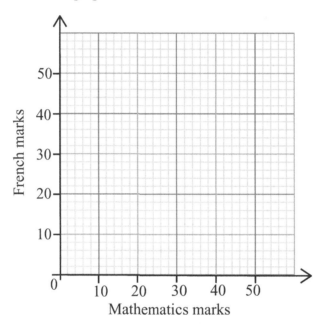

[3 marks]

b) Draw a line of best fit on your graph and circle any outliers.

[2 marks]

c) Describe the type of correlation this data shows.

....

[1 mark]

d) A pupil was absent for the French exam but scored 34 in the Maths exam.
    What mark would you expect the pupil to have got in French?

....

[2 marks]

7) The number of letters in each student's name in a class are listed below.
    One number is missing.

    7   3   9   5   4   3   8   6   5   6   4   3   8   10   7   6   8

    The mean number of letters in each student's name is 6.
    Find the missing number from the list.

....

[3 marks]

Summary Questions

You know what's coming by now — here are some questions to check it's all sunk in.
- Try these questions and tick off each one when you get it right.
- When you've done all the questions for a topic and are completely happy, tick off the topic.

Probability (p.109-111) ☐

1) What does a probability of 1 mean? ☐

2) In a bag of sweets, there are 5 cola bottles, 2 jelly snakes, 3 chocolate buttons and 2 chocolate mice. Find the probability of randomly picking a cola bottle. ☐

3) In a game, you can either win or lose. If P(win) = 0.1, what is P(lose)? ☐

4) I have a spinner that is half black and half white. I spin it twice. Fill in the table on the right to show all the possible results. ☐

5) Write down the formula for experimental probability. ☐

		Second spin	
		Black	White
First spin	Black		BW
	White		

Recording and Sorting Data (p.112-114) ☐

6) What is discrete data? ☐

7) This frequency table shows the number of pieces of fruit people eat each day. How many people eat 3 pieces of fruit?

Pieces of Fruit	0	1	2	3	4
Frequency	8	20	17	9	3

8) Sort these numbers into a Venn diagram, using the groups 'prime numbers' and 'factors of 8': 1, 2, 3, 4, 5, 6, 7, 8, 9, 10, 11, 12 ☐

9) Write the letter of each shape in the correct place in the Carroll diagram. ☐

A B C D E F

	3 sides	Not 3 sides
All straight sides		
Not all straight sides		

Graphs and Charts (p.115-116) ☐

10) A pie chart is drawn, showing the answers given by 120 people in a survey. The angle for 'not even for £1000' is 30°. How many gave this answer? ☐

11) What do the heights of the bars in a bar chart show? ☐

12) Draw a bar chart to show the data in the table on the right. ☐

No. of holidays	Frequency
0	5
1	10
2	8
3	3

Mean, Median, Mode and Range (p.117) ☐

13) Find the mode, median, mean and range of this data: 2, 8, 7, 5, 11, 5, 4 ☐

14) Four numbers have a mean of 8. The first three numbers are 5, 7 and 8. What is the other number? ☐

Scatter Graphs (p.118) ☐

15) What type of correlation is shown on the scatter graph on the right? ☐

16) By drawing a line of best fit on the scatter graph, estimate the age of a person who spends 1.5 hours on the Internet per week. ☐

Hours on the Internet (per week) / Age

Glossary

We've gathered up some of the most important words you need to know here, so you can remind yourself what they're all about. Words in the definitions that are underlined have their own entry.

2D Shape
A shape with only two dimensions, e.g. width and height.

3D Shape
A solid shape with length, width and height.

Acute Angle
An angle less than 90°.

Allied Angles
Angles within a pair of parallel lines that add up to 180°.

Alternate Angles
Equal angles within a pair of parallel lines.

Approximation
A number that is not exact because it has been rounded or estimated.

Arc
Part of the circumference of a circle.

Area
The space inside a 2D shape.

Arithmetic Sequence
A number sequence where the terms increase or decrease by the same amount each time.

Axis
The vertical and horizontal lines on a graph that the coordinates are measured along. The plural is 'axes'.

Bar Chart
A chart where the heights of the bars show the frequency of each category.

Biased
Where something, e.g. a dice or a spinner, is unfair and more likely to land on one or more of its sides than others.

BODMAS
A way of describing the order that operations should be done in a calculation containing multiple operations.

Brackets
Symbols, such as (), used to group things together.

Cancelling Down
Dividing all the parts of a fraction or ratio by the same number to reduce it to a simpler form.

Carroll Diagram
A table which sorts data depending on whether it has a certain property or not.

Century
100 years.

Certain
Will definitely happen.

Chord
A line drawn across the inside of a circle.

Circumference
The distance around the outside of a circle (its perimeter).

Common Denominator
Fractions have a common denominator when their denominators are the same.

Common Factor
A number that divides exactly into two or more different numbers.

Common Multiple
A number that will divide by two or more different numbers.

Compasses
A tool used for drawing arcs to construct and bisect 2D shapes.

Congruent
The same shape and size.

Coordinates
A pair of numbers (x, y) that describe the position of a point on a grid or set of axes, e.g. (2, 3).

Correlation
The relationship between two things, usually shown by the points on a scatter graph. Correlation can be either positive or negative.

Corresponding Angles
Equal angles around a pair of parallel lines.

Cross-section
The 2D shape you get when you cut a 3D shape.

Cube (number)
The result of multiplying a number or letter by itself, then by itself again.

Cube Root
The inverse of cubing a number.

Cube (shape)
A 3D shape with 6 identical square faces.

Cuboid
A 3D shape with 3 pairs of matching rectangular faces.

Cylinder
A 3D shape with a circular cross-section that is the same all the way through.

Data
Pieces of information.

Decade
10 years.

Decimal
A number where tenths, hundredths and thousandths, etc. are written after a decimal point.

Decimal Place
The position of a digit to the right of the decimal point.

Denominator
The bottom number of a fraction.

Diameter
The length across a circle, going through the centre.

Digit
A number from 0 to 9.

Direct Proportion
When the ratio between two things stays the same. If you increase one thing, the other increases at the same rate.

Discrete Data
Data that is countable.

Distance

How far an object has travelled.

Divisor

The number that divides another number.

Edge

Part of a 3D shape, where two faces meet.

Enlargement

Changing an object's size but keeping the shape the same.

Equation

A collection of terms that contains an equals sign. E.g. $y = 2x + 3$.

Equilateral Triangle

A regular triangle, with three equal sides and three equal angles of 60°.

Estimate

An approximate value of a number, often the result of a calculation where rounded numbers have been used instead of the actual values.

Expected Frequency

How many times you'd expect an event to happen during a certain number of trials.

Experimental Probability

An estimate of how likely something is to happen based on the results of an experiment.

Expression

A collection of terms made up of numbers and letters, separated by + or – signs, that doesn't contain an equals or inequality sign.

Exterior Angle

The angle between a side of a polygon, and the line extended from a neighbouring side.

Face

A surface of a 3D shape.

Factor

A number that divides exactly into another number.

Factorise

Rewrite an expression by putting in brackets with a factor on the outside.

Fair

Where something, e.g. a dice or a spinner, is equally likely to land on any of its sides.

Formula

A rule written using algebra which can be used to work out a value.

Fraction

A part of a whole, written as one number on top of another.

Frequency

How many items are in a category.

Frequency Diagram

A bar chart that shows data from a frequency table.

Frequency Table

A table showing how many times each value in a set of data occurs.

Geometric Sequence

A number sequence where each term is found by multiplying or dividing the previous term by the same number.

Gradient

The steepness of a line — a measure of how much it slopes.

Highest Common Factor (HCF)

The highest number that can be divided exactly into a set of numbers.

Horizontal

A flat line that runs from left to right.

Hypotenuse

The longest side of a right-angled triangle.

Imperial Units

A non-metric set of units for measuring, including inches, feet, yards, ounces, pounds, stones, pints and gallons.

Impossible

Has no chance of happening.

Improper Fraction

A fraction where the numerator is greater than the denominator.

Inequality

A way of comparing the values of numbers. < means less than, > means greater than, ≤ means less than or equal to and ≥ means greater than or equal to.

Integer

A whole number, positive or negative (including zero).

Interior Angle

An angle within a polygon.

Inverse Operation

The opposite operation. E.g. subtraction is the inverse of addition.

Inverse Proportion

When one thing increases as another decreases. E.g. when one thing doubles in size, the other one halves.

Isosceles Triangle

A triangle with two equal sides and two equal angles.

Kite

A quadrilateral with two pairs of equal sides and one pair of equal angles.

Line Graph

A graph showing two things plotted against each other. The plotted points are joined with straight lines.

Line of Best Fit

A line drawn on a scatter graph which goes through the middle of the set of data points, passing as close to as many of the points as possible.

Line Symmetry

A shape has line symmetry if you can draw on a mirror line where one side of the shape is the exact reflection of the other.

Lowest Common Multiple (LCM)

The smallest number that's in the times tables of a group of numbers.

Mean

The average of a set of data, found by adding up all of the values and dividing by the number of values.

Median

The middle value when you put a set of data in size order.

Metric Units

A standard set of units for measuring, including mm, cm, m, km, g, kg, tonnes, ml and litres.

Millennium

1000 years.

Mirror Line

The line that a shape or object is reflected in.

Mixed Number

A number made up of a whole number part and a fraction part.

Mode

The most common value in a set of data.

Multiple

A value in a number's times table.

Negative

Any number less than zero.

Negative Correlation

As one thing on a scatter graph increases, the other decreases.

Net

A hollow 3D shape folded out flat.

No Correlation

The points plotted on a scatter graph are spread out and show no relation.

Numerator

The top number of a fraction.

Obtuse Angle

An angle greater than 90° but less than 180°.

Operation

Something you do to one or more numbers, such as add, subtract, multiply or divide.

Order of Rotational Symmetry

The number of positions, in one full turn, you can rotate a shape into so that it looks the same.

Origin

The point with coordinates (0, 0) on a graph. It's where the axes cross.

Outcome

A possible result of a probability trial.

Parabola

The shape a quadratic graph has — it is a symmetrical bucket shape.

Parallel Lines

Lines that are always the same distance apart and never meet.

Parallelogram

A quadrilateral with two pairs of equal parallel sides and two pairs of equal angles.

Percentage

'Per cent' means 'out of 100'. Percentage shows an amount as a number out of 100.

Percentage Change

The amount a value increases or decreases by, given as a percentage of the original value.

Perimeter

The total distance around the outside of a shape.

Perpendicular Lines

Two lines which cross at right angles.

Pi

The number 3.14159265..., written using the Greek letter π.

Pictogram

A chart that displays numbers of things using pictures.

Pie Chart

A chart where the angles of each sector are proportional to the frequency of each category.

Polygon

An enclosed 2D shape whose sides are all straight.

Positive

Any number greater than zero.

Positive Correlation

As one thing on a scatter graph increases, so does the other.

Power

A way of showing that a number or letter is being multiplied by itself a certain number of times. The power tells you how many of the number or letter to multiply together.

Prime Factor

A factor of a number that is a prime number.

Prime Number

A number that has no factors except itself and 1.

Prism

A 3D shape which is the same shape all the way through.

Probability

How likely it is that something will happen.

Product

The result when two things are multiplied together.

Protractor

A tool used for drawing and measuring angles.

Pythagoras' Theorem

A formula linking the lengths of the sides of a right-angled triangle. Pythagoras' theorem states that $a^2 + b^2 = c^2$, where c is the hypotenuse and a and b are the shorter sides.

Quadrant

A quarter of a graph split by the x- and y-axes.

Quadratic

An equation or expression which contains an x^2 term, but no higher powers of x.

Quadrilateral

A four-sided polygon.

Radius

The distance from the centre to the edge of a circle.

Range

The difference between the highest value and the lowest value in a set of data.

Ratio

The amount of one thing compared to another, written e.g. 2 : 1.

Reciprocal

The reciprocal of a number is 1 divided by it. For a fraction, the reciprocal is found by swapping the numerator and the denominator.

Rectangle

A quadrilateral with two pairs of equal sides and four right angles (90°).

Reflection

A transformation where a shape is flipped in a mirror line. OR a mirror image of another shape, with every point the same distance from the mirror line as in the original shape.

Reflex Angle

An angle greater than 180° but less than 360°.

Regular Polygon

A polygon with sides of equal length and angles that are all equal.

Rhombus

A quadrilateral with four equal sides (opposite sides are parallel) and two pairs of equal angles.

Right Angle

An angle of 90°.

Right-Angled Triangle

A triangle with one angle of 90°.

Rotation

Turning an object, either clockwise or anticlockwise, through a given angle around a given point.

Rotational Symmetry

A shape has rotational symmetry if you can rotate it so that it looks exactly the same from a different position.

Rounding

Approximating a number (e.g. writing it with fewer decimal places or as a multiple of 10, 100, etc.)

Scale Factor

The amount each length increases by in an enlargement.

Scale (measuring)

The number line on a measuring device, which you read to measure something.

Scalene Triangle

A triangle with all three sides and angles different.

Scatter Graph

A graph showing two things plotted against each other. The plotted points are never joined with a line, but the graph may show a line of best fit.

Sector

A wedge-shaped area of a circle.

Segment

The area of a circle when you cut along a chord.

Sequence

A pattern of numbers or shapes that follow a certain rule.

Significant Figures

The first significant figure is the first non-zero digit of a number. Each number that follows after is an additional significant figure.

Similar

When two objects have the same shape but different sizes.

Simplify

Make something simpler, e.g. by dividing by common factors or collecting like terms.

Simultaneous Equations

Two equations with two unknowns that can be solved at the same time.

Solve

To find the value(s) of the unknown(s) that make equations true.

Speed

How fast an object is travelling.

Sphere

A perfectly round 3D shape.

Square-Based Pyramid

A 3D shape made of a square base, and 4 triangular faces that meet at a point.

Square (number)

The result of multiplying a number or letter by itself.

Square Root

The inverse of squaring a number.

Square (shape)

A regular quadrilateral, with four equal sides and four right angles (90°).

Standard Form

A way of writing very small or very large numbers in the form $A \times 10^n$.

Substitute

To replace something in a term with something else, e.g. a letter with a number.

Sum

The total of some numbers.

Surface Area

The total area of all the faces of a 3D shape added together.

Symmetry

A shape has symmetry if it can be reflected or rotated to give the same shape.

Tangent

A straight line that just touches the outside of a circle.

Term (of an expression)

A number, a letter or collection of numbers or letters multiplied/ divided together.

Tetrahedron

A 3D shape with 4 triangular faces (also known as a triangle-based pyramid).

Transformation

Changing the size, orientation or position of an object.

Translation

Changing the position of an object by sliding it horizontally and vertically.

Trapezium

A quadrilateral with one pair of parallel sides.

Triangle

A three-sided polygon.

Triangular Prism

A prism with a triangular cross-section.

Venn Diagram

A diagram that sorts things into different groups, using circles to represent the groups.

Vertex

The corner of a 2D or 3D shape.

Vertical

A line going straight up and down.

Volume

The amount of space that a 3D shape occupies.

x-axis

The horizontal axis of a graph.

y-axis

The vertical axis of a graph.

Answers

Section 1 — Numbers

Page 3 — Calculating Tips
1) a) 1   b) 14   c) 14
2) a) 21   b) 2   c) 4

Page 4 — Calculating Tips
1) 10

Page 5 — Calculating Tips
1) a) 50   Check: 50 – 16 = 34
            or 50 – 34 = 16
   b) 49   Check: 49 + 59 = 108
            or 59 + 49 = 108
   c) 161   Check: 161 ÷ 7 = 23
            or 161 ÷ 23 = 7
   d) 26   Check: 26 × 6 = 156
            6 × 26 = 156
2) a) 5   b) 5

Page 6 — Place Value
1) a) Nine million, nine hundred and five thousand, two hundred and eighty-five.
   b) Six million, fifty-four thousand, two hundred and three.
2) a) six tenths
   b) seven thousandths

Page 7 — Ordering Numbers
1) 318, 107, 35, –5, –6, –16, –24, –115
2) a) 30 000 > 29 950
   b) 0.005 < 0.045

Page 8 — Addition and Subtraction
1) a) 797   b) 852   c) 18.45
2) 12.35 seconds

Page 9 — Multiplying by 10, 100, etc.
1) a) 64   b) 85 200   c) 88.5
   d) 270   e) 1920
2) 3200

Page 10 — Dividing by 10, 100, etc.
1) a) 0.859   b) 356.98
   c) 0.06752   d) 104
2) £67.98

Page 11 — Multiplying Without a Calculator
1) a) 3776   b) 1554   c) 32 576

Page 12 — Dividing Without a Calculator
1) a) 16   b) 22   c) 12.5
2) 6 gummy worms

Page 13 — Multiplying and Dividing with Decimals
1) a) 120.54   b) 2.598   c) 1.02
2) 64   3) 640

Page 14 — Negative Numbers
1) a) 5   b) –15   c) 18   d) –3
2) 14.1 °C

Page 15 — Prime Numbers
1) 73, 83

Page 16 — Multiples, Factors and Prime Factors
1) a) 15, 30, 45, 60, 75, 90, 105, 120
   b) 1, 2, 4, 8, 16, 32, 64
2) 60, 72
3) a) $2 \times 2 \times 3 \times 5 \times 5$
   b) $2^2 \times 3 \times 5^2$

Page 17 — Common Multiples and Factors
1) 36   2) 16

Page 18 — Fractions, Decimals and Percentages
1) a) $\frac{4}{5}$ b) $\frac{1}{25}$ c) $\frac{23}{100}$ d) $\frac{999}{1000}$
2) a) $\frac{3}{9}$ b) 0.7
3) $\frac{1}{5}$, 0.5, 55%

Page 19 — Fractions
1) a) $\frac{5}{7}$ b) $\frac{1}{4}$
2) $\frac{2}{3}$ 3) $6\frac{1}{7}$

Page 20 — Fractions
1) $\frac{7}{10}$ 2) a) $\frac{2}{9}$ b) $\frac{6}{12}$ or $\frac{1}{2}$
3) $\frac{63}{6}$ or $\frac{21}{2}$
4) a) $\frac{161}{15}$ or $10\frac{11}{15}$
   b) $\frac{118}{104}$ or $\frac{59}{52}$ or $1\frac{7}{52}$

Page 21 — Fractions
1) 12 m   2) 295   3) $\frac{7}{8}$

Page 22 — Percentage Basics
1) a) 196.95   b) 623
2) 75%

Page 23 — Rounding Numbers and Estimating
1) a) 23.6   b) 6.79
2) a) 135.0   b) 4.90

Page 24 — Rounding Numbers and Estimating
1) a) 18   b) 51 700
2) 0.26   3) E.g. 15 × 30 = 450

Page 25 — Powers and Roots
1) Squares: 4, 9, 16, 25, 36, 49, 64, 81
   Cubes: 8, 27, 64
2) a) 82   b) 11   c) 8

Page 26 — Standard Form
1) a) 1.9×10^7 b) 6.57×10^4

Page 27 — Warm-Up Questions
1) a) 15   b) 6   c) 2
2) –1.4, –0.76, 0.23, 1.23, 2.03
3) a) 43.4   b) 138   c) 70
4) a) 432   b) 19   c) 44.82
5) 24
6) a) $\frac{5}{6}$ b) $\frac{1}{36}$
   c) $\frac{3}{20}$ d) $\frac{7}{12}$
7) a) 24   b) £600   c) 450

8) a) 4170   b) 4200   c) 4000
9) a) 5   b) 12   c) 4
10) a) 45 200   b) 7.08×10^5

Pages 28-30 — Practice Questions
2) E.g. Convert all of the numbers to decimals: 0.12, 17% = 0.17, $\frac{1}{20} = \frac{5}{100} = 0.05$, $\frac{13}{100} = 0.13$, 9% = 0.09, $\frac{9}{50} = \frac{18}{100} = 0.18$ *[1 mark]*
   Now order the decimals from smallest to largest:
   0.05, 0.09, 0.12, 0.13, 0.17, 0.18 *[1 mark]*
   Put the numbers back into their original form:
   $\frac{1}{20}$, 9%, 0.12, $\frac{13}{100}$, 17%, $\frac{9}{50}$ *[1 mark]*
   [3 marks available — as above]
3) a) 5 – 24 + 5 *[1 mark]*
   = –19 + 5 = –14 *[1 mark]*
   [2 marks available — as above]
   b) $\frac{55 \div 2}{20 - 9} = \frac{110}{11}$ *[1 mark]*
   = 10 *[1 mark]*
   [2 marks available — as above]
4) a) First calculate 178 × 5:
   ```
        1 7 8
      ×     5
      ─────────
        8 9 0
          3 4
   ```
   17.8 has 1 digit after the decimal point, so 17.8 × 5 = 89.0 = 89
   [2 marks available — 1 mark for a correct method, 1 mark for the correct answer]
   b)
   ```
        8 9 .1 4 4
      −   5 . 7 0
      ─────────────
        3 . 7 4
   ```
   [2 marks available — 1 mark for a correct method, 1 mark for the correct answer]
5)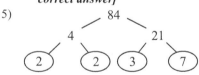
   So $84 = 2 \times 2 \times 3 \times 7 = 2^2 \times 3 \times 7$
   [2 marks available — 1 mark for a correct method, 1 mark for the correct answer]
6) a) $61.24 \div 5.92 \approx 60 \div 6 = 10$ *[1 mark]*
   b) $121.6 \times 0.49 \approx 120 \div 2 = 60$
   [1 mark]
   c) Round each number to something that's easy to work with:
   $\frac{38.4 \times 28.2}{6.17 \times 2.02} \approx \frac{40 \times 30}{6 \times 2}$
   $= \frac{1200}{12} = 100$
   [2 marks available — 1 mark for a correct method, 1 mark for the correct answer]

7) a) 10% of 40 = 40 ÷ 10 = 4
   5% of 40 = 10% ÷ 2 = 4 ÷ 2 = 2
   So 15% of 40 = 4 + 2 = 6
   *[2 marks available — 1 mark for
   a correct method, 1 mark for the
   correct answer]*

   b) $\frac{7}{9}$ of 45 = 45 ÷ 9 × 7 = 5 × 7 = 35
   *[2 marks available — 1 mark for
   a correct method, 1 mark for the
   correct answer]*

8) £4800 as a percentage of £12 000
   = $\frac{4800}{12\,000}$ × 100 = 40%
   *[2 marks available — 1 mark for a
   correct method, 1 mark for the correct
   answer]*

9) a) 11.92 *[1 mark]*
   b) 4.34 *[1 mark]*
   c) 4.57 *[1 mark]*

10) a) $\frac{2}{7}$ of 21 = 21 ÷ 7 × 2
      = 3 × 2 = 6 blue marbles
   $\frac{1}{3}$ of 21 = 21 ÷ 3 = 7 red marbles
   21 – 6 – 7 = 8 green marbles
   *[3 marks available — 1 mark
   for finding the number of blue
   marbles, 1 mark for finding the
   number of red marbles, 1 mark for
   the correct answer]*

   b) 15 ÷ $\frac{3}{4}$ = 15 × $\frac{4}{3}$ = $\frac{60}{3}$ = 20 bags
   *[3 marks available — 1 mark for a
   correct method to divide fractions,
   1 mark for multiplying correctly,
   1 mark for the correct answer]*

11) £1.5 million = £1 500 000
   and 3 × 10⁴ = 30 000
   £1 500 000 ÷ 30 000 = £50
   *[3 marks available — 1 mark for
   converting between standard form
   and ordinary numbers, 1 mark for a
   correct method, 1 mark for the correct
   answer]*
   *You could also have written both numbers
   in standard form.*

Page 31 — Summary Questions
1) a) 9   b) 8   c) 1
2) a) 15   b) 6
3) –11.8, –0.51, –0.09, 0.001,
   0.02, 0.9, 23.91, 54
4) Day 2
5) a) 611   b) 596   c) 2.673
6) a) 122.3   b) 15 120
   c) 0.675   d) 0.0062
7) a) 2489   b) 48
   c) 310.08   d) 5.05
8) a) –2   b) –14
   c) 56   d) –9
9) a) 41, 43, 47   b) 83, 89
10) a) 13, 26, 39, 52, 65
    b) 1, 2, 3, 4, 6, 9, 12, 18, 36
11) 2 × 2 × 2 × 3 × 3 × 7 or 2³ × 3² × 7
12) 4
13) a) $\frac{6}{10}$ or $\frac{3}{5}$ and 60%
    b) $\frac{65}{100}$ or $\frac{13}{20}$ and 0.65

14) E.g. $\frac{6}{10}$ and $\frac{9}{15}$
15) a) $\frac{5}{8}$ b) $\frac{2}{5}$ c) $\frac{5}{9}$
16) a) $\frac{8}{9}$ b) $\frac{1}{5}$
    c) $\frac{7}{12}$ d) $\frac{20}{33}$
17) a) $1\frac{7}{9}$ (or $\frac{16}{9}$)   b) $1\frac{5}{8}$ (or $\frac{13}{8}$)
    c) $10\frac{1}{8}$ (or $\frac{81}{8}$)   d) –22
18) a) 120   b) 210
    c) 11.7   d) £171
19) a) $\frac{1}{26}$ b) 4%
20) a) 164.4   b) 765 440
21) a) 76 000   b) 30
22) a) 1000   b) 10   c) 1000
23) 16, 49, 121
24) a) 15.8   b) 14
25) a) 200 000 000   b) 4.3 × 10⁶
26) 56 000 000

Section 2 — Algebra

Page 32 — Algebra —
Simplifying Terms
1) a) 3a   b) 8d   c) 6x + 2y
2) a) –12f   b) 25x   c) 3a + b

Page 33 — Algebra —
Simplifying Terms
1) a) d^5 b) 16ef
   c) p^{10} d) 4j
2) a) 4   b) 10
   c) $3c^2$ d) $4e^2f^4$

Page 34 — Algebra — Multiplying
Out Brackets
1) a) 8 – 2x   b) 12x – 18y
2) 1 – 2x
3) a) 8h – dh   b) $6j – 2j^2$
   c) $3ab^2 – 6b^3$

Page 35 — Algebra — Factorising
and Proof
1) a) 2(2 – 5r)   b) 2(3x + y)
   c) 6(5s + 2)
   d) –8(5 + 3t) or 8(–5 – 3t)
2) a) a(a + 4)   b) 3b(3b – 1)
   c) $3cd(3c + 4d^2)$

Page 36 — Solving Equations
1) a) x = 3   b) x = 11
   c) x = 3   d) x = 21
2) a) x = $\frac{3}{4}$ b) x = $\frac{5}{3}$ or $1\frac{2}{3}$
3) a) x = 20   b) x = 1

Page 37 — Solving Equations
1) x = –10   2) x = $\frac{1}{2}$ 3) x = 3

Page 38 — Solving Equations
1) x = $\frac{8}{3}$ or $2\frac{2}{3}$ 2) x = $\frac{3}{4}$
3) a) x = 3 or x = –3
   b) x = 5 or x = –5
   c) x = 1 or x = –1

Page 39 — Using Expressions
and Formulas
1) a) C = 46   b) a = $\frac{C - 2b}{5}$

Page 40 — Making Formulas
from Words
1) 3 hours

Page 41 — Inequalities
1) 1, 2, 3, 4
2)

Page 42 — Number Patterns
and Sequences
1) Subtract 6 from the previous term
   — the next term is 14.

Page 43 — Number Patterns
and Sequences
1) a) Multiply term number
   by 8 and add 7.
   b) 231
2) 12n – 9

Page 44 — Simultaneous Equations
1) x = 6, y = 2
2) a) 3x + 2y = 26, 4x + y = 23
   b) x = 4, y = 7

Page 45 — Warm-Up Questions
1) a) 2x + 3y   b) 3t – 5s
   c) $30b^2$ d) 10
2) a) 12a + 6   b) –12 + 18   c) 2 – 3z
3) a) 5(x + 2)
   b) –3(m + 4) or 3(–m – 4)
   c) $3(2 – 3p^2)$
4) a) x = 2   b) x = $\frac{7}{2}$ c) x = 12
5) a) –12   b) 14   c) 6
6) –1, 0, 1, 2, 3, 4, 5
7) a) 33 and 40   b) –8 and –14
   c) 15 and 7.5
8) 3n + 4
9) x = 2, y = –3

Pages 46-48 — Practice Questions
2) a) 6x – 4y – 7x + 5y = 6x – 7x – 4y + 5y
      = –x + y
   *[2 marks available — 1 mark for
   a correct method, 1 mark for the
   correct answer]*
   b) $3a^2 × 2ab = 3 × 2 × a^2 × a × b = 6a^3b$
   *[2 marks available — 1 mark for
   a correct method, 1 mark for the
   correct answer]*
3) a) 3(5x – 1) + 2x = (15x – 3) + 2x
      = 17x – 3
   *[2 marks available — 1 mark for
   a correct method, 1 mark for the
   correct answer]*
   b) 16 – 4(2a – 3) = 16 – (8a – 12)
      = 16 – 8a + 12 = 28 – 8a
   *[2 marks available — 1 mark for
   a correct method, 1 mark for the
   correct answer]*
   c) $4y^2 – y(5 – 2y) = 4y^2 – (5y – 2y^2)$
      $= 4y^2 – 5y + 2y^2 = 6y^2 – 5y$
   *[2 marks available — 1 mark for
   a correct method, 1 mark for the
   correct answer]*
4) a) 6y – 3 = 3(2y – 1)
   *[2 marks available — 1 mark for
   taking out a factor of 3, 1 mark for
   the correct answer]*

b) $8a + 28b = 4(2a + 7b)$
[2 marks available — 1 mark for taking out a factor of 4, 1 mark for the correct answer]
c) $5a^2 - 10ab = 5a(a - 2b)$
[2 marks available — 1 mark for taking out a factor of 5a, 1 mark for the correct answer]

5)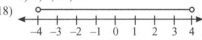
[2 marks available — 1 mark for an open circle at 1, 1 mark for a solid circle at 7]

6) a) $4x + 7 = 15$
Subtract 7 from both sides: $4x = 8$
Divide both sides by 4: $x = 2$
[2 marks available — 1 mark for a correct method, 1 mark for the correct answer]
b) $\frac{3x - 1}{5} = 4$
Multiply both sides by 5 to get rid of the fraction: $3x - 1 = 20$
Add 1 to both sides: $3x = 21$
Divide both sides by 3: $x = 7$
[2 marks available — 1 mark for a correct method, 1 mark for the correct answer]
c) $\frac{2x + 1}{3} - \frac{x - 3}{2} = 2$
Multiply every term by 3:
$2x + 1 - \frac{3(x - 3)}{2} = 6$ *[1 mark]*
Then multiply every term by 2:
$2(2x + 1) - 3(x - 3) = 12$ *[1 mark]*
$4x + 2 - 3x + 9 = 12$ *[1 mark]*
$x + 11 = 12$ *[1 mark]*
$x = 12 - 11$ so $x = 1$ *[1 mark]*
[5 marks available — as above]

7) a) To get from one term to the next, you add 2, so you multiply the term number by 2. *[1 mark]* Then to get from 2 × the term number to the term, you add 5. *[1 mark]*
So the 50th term is:
$2 \times 50 + 5 = 105$ *[1 mark]*
[3 marks available — as above]
b) To get from one term to the next, you subtract 4, so you multiply the term number by –4. *[1 mark]* Then to get from –4 × the term number to the term, you add 15. *[1 mark]*
So the 50th term is:
$-4 \times 50 + 15 = -185$ *[1 mark]*
[3 marks available — as above]

8) Let x represent the number Jan is thinking of. Then $(2x + 3)^2 = 81$.
Take the square root of both sides:
$2x + 3 = 9$ or $2x + 3 = -9$
If $2x + 3 = 9$, $2x = 6$ and $x = 3$
If $2x + 3 = -9$, $2x = -12$ and $x = -6$.
Jan is thinking of a positive number, so the number she is thinking of is 3.
[3 marks available — 1 mark for forming an equation, 1 mark for a correct method to solve, 1 mark for the correct answer]

9) $3V = \pi r^2 h$ *[1 mark]*
$\frac{3V}{\pi r^2} = h$ *[1 mark]*
[2 marks available — as above]

10) $4x + 5y = 6$ ①
$2x - y = -4$ ② *[1 mark]*
$2 \times$ ②: $4x - 2y = -8$ ③ *[1 mark]*
① – ③: $5y - (-2y) = 6 - (-8)$
$7y = 14$ *[1 mark]*
so $y = 2$ *[1 mark]*
Substitute $y = 2$ into ② to find x:
$2x - 2 = -4$, so $2x = -2$, so $x = -1$
The solution is $x = -1$, $y = 2$ *[1 mark]*
[5 marks available — as above]

Page 49 — Summary Questions

1) a) $4a$ b) $9b$ c) $6d + e$
2) a) g^3 b) $a^2 b^2$
   c) $8m^3 n^3$ d) $\frac{g}{4}$
3) a) $3v + 24$ b) $-14w - 35$
4) $12y - 18$
5) a) $3(x + 3)$ b) $7(x + 3y)$
6) a) $g(5g - 2)$ b) $6h(1 + 2h)$
   c) $2jk(2k^4 + 9j^2)$
7) $4(5 - 2y) + 3(y - 10)$
   $= 20 - 8y + 3y - 30$
   $= -5y - 10 = -5(y + 2)$ ∎
8) $5x(x - 2) - x(5 - x)$
   $= 5x^2 - 10x - 5x + x^2$
   $= 6x^2 - 15x = 3(2x^2 - 5x)$
   If x is an integer, $(2x^2 - 5x)$ is an integer, so $3(2x^2 - 5x) = 3 \times$ an integer, so it's a multiple of 3. ∎
9) a) $x = 7$ b) $x = 7$
   c) $x = 3$ d) $x = 6$
10) a) $x = \frac{14}{5}$ b) $x = 4$ c) $x = 2$
11) $x = 13$
12) a) $x = 6$ or $x = -6$
    b) $x = 8$ or $x = -8$
13) 13
14) $q = 9$
15) $P = 7s + 4f$
16) a) $b = \frac{a - 2}{3}$ b) $b = 3(a + 7)$
    c) $b = \frac{4a + 1}{5}$
17) a) 1, 2, 3, 4, 5, 6
    b) 8, 9, 10, 11
18)
19) a) 26 — Add 6 to the previous term.
    b) 243 — Multiply the previous term by 3.
    c) 59 — Subtract 9 from the previous term.
    d) 25 — Square the term number, or increase the number you add to the previous term by 2 each time.
    e) 21 — Add the two previous terms together.
    f) 125 — Cube the term number.
20) Multiply the term number by 6 and subtract 3.
21) $2n + 3$
22) 325
23) $x = 2, y = 5$

Section 3 — Graphs

Page 50 — X and Y Coordinates

1)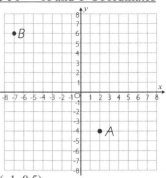
2) $(-1, 0.5)$

Page 51 — Straight Line Graphs

1) a) $x = 2$ b) $y = 4$
2) A line through the origin that slopes steeply downhill.

Page 52 — Plotting Straight Line Graphs

1) a) E.g.

x	0	1	2
y	4	2	0

b)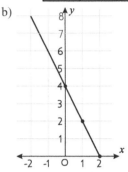

Page 53 — Plotting Straight Line Graphs

1) a) When $x = 0$, $y = 2$ and when $y = 0$, $x = -1$
b)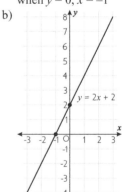

Page 54 — Reading Off Graphs

1) $y = 2.4$

Page 55 — Conversion Graphs

1) 2 inches

Page 56 — Solving Simultaneous Equations

1) a)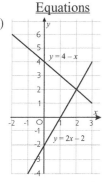

b) $x = 2$ and $y = 2$

Page 57 — Quadratic and Reciprocal Graphs

1) a)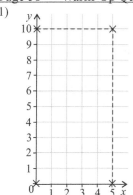

b) $x = -1$, $y = 4$, and $x = 3$, $y = 12$.

Page 58 — Warm-Up Questions

1)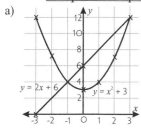

The coordinates of the fourth point are (5, 10).

2) (3, 5)

3) a) 5   b) −25
   c) 155   d) −295

4) Distance

5)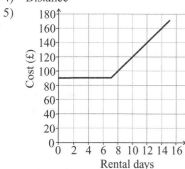

6) The solution is found at the point where the two lines cross.

7) It contains an x^2 term and no higher power of x.

8) a)

x	−8	−4	−2	−1	1	2	4	8
y	−1	−2	−4	−8	8	4	2	1

b)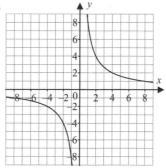

Pages 59-61 — Practice Questions

2) a) 3 km *[1 mark]*
   b) The woman is running slowest when the gradient is shallowest but not flat. This is between 13:45 and 14:45.
   [2 marks available — 1 mark for identifying the shallowest gradient as the slowest running, 1 mark for correct time interval]

3) a) & b)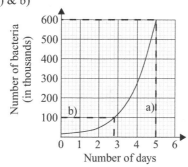

   a) 600 000 bacteria (see graph above)
   [2 marks available — 1 mark for a correct method, 1 mark for correct answer]
   b) 2.8 days (see graph above)
   [2 marks available — 1 mark for a correct method, 1 mark for correct answer]

4) a)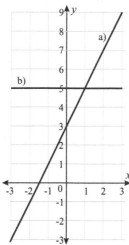

   [3 marks available — 3 marks for a fully correct graph, otherwise 2 marks for correct working, or 1 mark for an attempt at working]
   b) See graph in part a) *[1 mark]*
   c) (1, 5) *[1 mark]*

5) a) + b) E.g.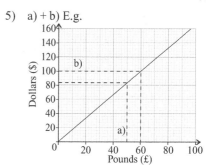

   a) $84
   [2 marks available — 1 mark for a correct method, 1 mark for the correct answer]
   b) $500 isn't on the graph, so choose a different value to use instead. E.g. from the graph, $100 ≈ £60. So $500 = £60 × 5 = £300
   [3 marks available — 1 mark for reading a sensible value off the graph, 1 mark for a correct method to find $500, 1 mark for the correct answer]

6) a) Read off the coordinates at the point where the lines $y = x + 4$ and $y = 4x - 2$ cross: $x = 2$, $y = 6$ *[1 mark]*
   b) Read off the coordinates at the point where the lines $y = x + 4$ and $y = 4 - 2x$ cross: $x = 0$, $y = 4$ *[1 mark]*

7) a)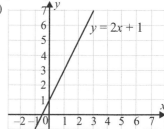

   [3 marks available — 3 marks for a fully correct graph, otherwise 2 marks for correct working, or 1 mark for an attempt at working]
   b)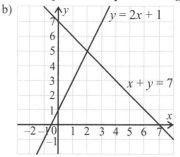

   [3 marks available — 3 marks for a fully correct graph, otherwise 2 marks for correct working, or 1 mark for an attempt at working]
   c) The x- and y-values that satisfy the simultaneous equations are the coordinates of the point where the two lines cross, so $x = 2$ and $y = 5$. *[1 mark]*

8) a) Draw up a table of values, e.g.:

x	–3	–2	–1	0	1	2	3
y	8	–2	–8	–10	–8	–2	8

Plot these values on the graph and draw a smooth curve:

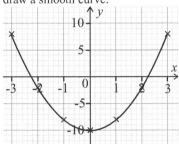

[4 marks available — 1 mark for a correct table of values, 2 marks for plotting all the points correctly, 1 mark for joining the points with a smooth curve]
Deduct 1 mark for plotting at least one point incorrectly.

b) Plot $y = 2x – 2$ on the graph:

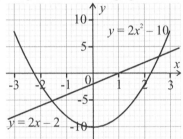

Read off x-values where the two lines cross to find the solutions to the equation: $x \approx -1.6$ and $x \approx 2.6$
[5 marks available — 1 mark for a correct method to plot the graph of $y = 2x – 2$, 1 mark for $y = 2x – 2$ plotted correctly, 1 mark for attempting to read x-values at the points where the two lines intersect, 1 mark for each correct value of x]

Page 62 — Summary Questions
1) $A(2, 2)$ $B(3, -2)$
   $C(-2, -3)$ $D(-2, 1)$
2) $(-2, -1)$
3) $(2.5, 0)$
4) a) E.g. $(4, 1)$ b) E.g. $(1, 2)$
5) $(3, 1)$
6) E.g. $x = 3$ and $x = 5$
7) a) Neither
   b) Downhill
8)

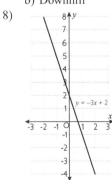

9) When $x = 0$, $y = 10$ and when $y = 0$, $x = 5$

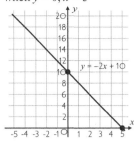

10) Draw a straight line from one axis to the graph, then draw a straight line down or across to the other axis.
11) a) On his way home.
    b) 15 minutes
12) a) 300 euros   b) 500 pounds
13)

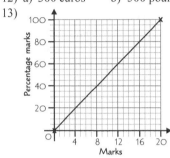

14)

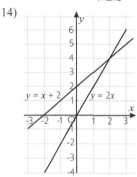

$x = 2$ and $y = 4$
15) Two symmetrical curves — one in the top right quadrant and one in the bottom left quadrant.
16) a)

x	–3	–2	–1	0	1	2	3
y	6	1	–2	–3	–2	1	6

b), c)

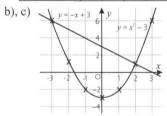

d) $x = 2$ and $y = 1$
   $x = -3$ and $y = 6$

Section 4 — Ratio, Proportion and Rates of Change

Page 63 — Ratios
1) a) $1 : 9$ b) $2 : 5$ c) $5 : 3$

Page 64 — Ratios
1) 35 litres
2) 126
3) $4 : 3$

Page 65 — Ratios
1) £240

Page 66 — Direct Proportion
1) 39   2) 9 kg
3) 378 g oats, 180 g butter, 150 g sugar

Page 67 — Inverse Proportion
1) 4.5 hours   2) 6 days

Page 68 — Percentage Change
1) a) $15 000   b) 75%
2) 6.25%

Page 69 — Percentage Change
1) 3150 m   2) 18 °C

Page 70 — Metric and Imperial Units
1) a) 35 mm   b) 2800 cm³   c) 4500 kg
2) a) 20 kg   b) 150 cm   c) 12.5 miles

Page 71 — Converting Units
1) 4.2 cm, 44 mm, 0.5 m
2) a) 41.6 km   b) 41 600 m
   c) 4 160 000 cm

Page 72 — More Conversions
1) a) 2400 mm³   b) 40 m²
2) 96 km/h

Page 73 — Reading Scales and Estimating
1) 12.5 ml
2) a) cm   b) kg   c) km

Page 74 — Time
1) 3 months 13 days

Page 75 — Speed
1) a) 12 km/h   b) 15 km/h

Page 76 — Warm-Up Questions
1) a) $1 : 5$ b) $3 : 5$ c) $3 : 20$
2) $1 : 4.5$
3) 25 sweets
4) 160 minutes (or 2 hours 40 minutes)
5) £400
6) £750
7) 10 lb, 5.5 kg, 7000 g
8) 240 000 cm³
9) a) metres   b) kilograms
10) 2 hours 25 minutes
11) 15 km

Pages 77-79 — Practice Questions
2) a) 7.6 *[1 mark]*
   b)
   [1 mark]
3) 1 calculator costs £35 ÷ 14 = £2.50.
   22 calculators cost £2.50 × 22 = £55.
   [2 marks available — 1 mark for a correct method, 1 mark for the correct answer]
4) a) Divide both sides by 5.
   $15 : 20 = 3 : 4$
   [2 marks available — 1 mark for a correct method, 1 mark for the correct answer]
   b) Convert 8 cm into mm, then divide both sides by 16.
   $80 \text{ mm} : 32 \text{ mm} = 5 : 2$
   [2 marks available — 1 mark for a correct method, 1 mark for the correct answer]
   You could divide in stages, e.g. divide both sides by 8 first, and then by 2.

c) Divide all three parts by 4.
$16 : 12 : 24 = 4 : 3 : 6$
[2 marks available — 1 mark for a correct method, 1 mark for the correct answer]

5) a) Conversion factor = 1000.
There will be more millilitres than litres, so multiply.
$7.2 \times 1000 = 7200$ ml *[1 mark]*
b) Conversion factor = 100.
There will be fewer m^2 than cm^2, and you're converting areas, so you need to divide twice.
$60\,000 \div 100 \div 100 = 6$ m^2.
[2 marks available — 1 mark for a correct method, 1 mark for the correct answer]

6) Total parts = $5 + 3 + 2 = 10$ *[1 mark]*
1 part = $50 \div 10 = 5$ badges *[1 mark]*
Shaun gets 5 parts:
$5 \times 5 = 25$ badges *[1 mark]*
[3 marks available — as above]

7) a) 600 ml of olive oil is 4 parts, so 1 part = 600 ml $\div 4 = 150$ ml.
[2 marks available — 1 mark for a correct method, 1 mark for the correct answer]
b) Total parts = $4 + 1 = 5$
1 part = $1.25 \div 5 = 0.25$
4 parts = $0.25 \times 4 = 1$ litre
[3 marks available — 1 mark for finding the total number of parts, 1 mark for the value of 1 part, 1 mark for the correct answer]

8) $\dfrac{60 - 51}{60} \times 100 = 15\%$
[2 marks available — 1 mark for a correct method, 1 mark for the correct answer]

9) 500 ml bottle: £1.50 = 150p, so you get $500 \div 150 = 3.33...$ ml of orange juice per penny *[1 mark]*.
1.2 litre bottle: 1.2 litres = 1200 ml, £3.40 = 340p, so you get:
$1200 \div 340 = 3.52...$ ml of orange juice per penny *[1 mark]*. The more orange juice per penny, the better the value for money. So the best value for money bottle is the 1.2 litre bottle *[1 mark]*.
[3 marks available — as above]

10) It would take 1 person $8 \times 2 = 16$ hours to paint the same mural. So it would take 5 people $16 \div 5 = 3.2$ hours to paint the same mural.
[2 marks available — 1 mark for a correct method, 1 mark for the correct answer]

11) 165 cm is 120% of the height of the sunflower last week. 1% of the height last week = $165 \div 120 = 1.375$
100% of height last week = $1.375 \times 100 = 137.5$ cm
[4 marks available — 1 mark for finding what percentage of the original value 165 cm is, 1 mark for a correct method to find 1% of the original value, 1 mark for correct 1%, 1 mark for the correct answer]

12) The car travels $35 + 100 = 135$ m over the whole journey *[1 mark]*. The time taken in the first part of the journey is distance $\div$ speed $= 35 \div 7 = 5$ seconds *[1 mark]*. So the total time for the journey is $5 + 10 = 15$ seconds *[1 mark]*. So the average speed of the car over the whole journey = distance $\div$ time $= 135 \div 15 = 9$ m/s *[1 mark]*.
[4 marks available — as above]

Page 80 — Summary Questions
1) a) $7:8$ b) $3:2$ c) $8:7$
2) $1:3.6$
3) 50 DVDs
4) £105
5) £1.25
6) a) 15 minutes   b) 1 hour
7) £70
8) 16%
9) a) 1000   b) 2.5   c) 1.75
10) 10 000 g
11) a) 50 miles   b) 75 cm
12) a) 0.2 m   b) 60 cm^2
13) 180 000 mm^3
14) 43.2 km/h
15) 27.5 kg
16) E.g. grams (g)
17) 1 litre
18) 280 minutes
19) 75 km
20) 4 km/h
21) 6.25 km/h

Section 5 — Geometry and Measures

Page 81 — Symmetry
1) 1   2) 2

Page 82 — Quadrilaterals
1) Kite

Page 83 — Triangles and Regular Polygons
1) 20 lines of symmetry, order of rotational symmetry = 20

Page 84 — Perimeter and Area
1) 4 m and 3 m
2) 40 cm^2

Page 85 — Area of Compound Shapes
1) 45 cm^2

Page 86 — Circles
1) Circumference = 62.8 mm (1 d.p.)
Area = 314.2 mm^2 (1 d.p.)
2) 8.74 cm (3 s.f.)

Page 87 — Circle Problems
1)

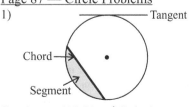

Tangent, Chord, Segment

2) Area = 137.44 cm^2 (2 d.p.)
Perimeter = 48.33 cm (2 d.p.)
3) 15.5 cm^2 (1 d.p.)

Page 88 — 3D Shapes
1) a) (Regular) tetrahedron
b) Faces = 4, edges = 6

Page 89 — Nets and Surface Area
1) 96 cm^2

Page 90 — Nets and Surface Area
1) E.g.

2) 12 cm^2

Page 91 — Volume
1) 168 cm^3

Page 92 — Angle Basics
1) a) obtuse   b) reflex   c) acute

Page 93 — Geometry Rules
1) $x = 25°$

Page 94 — Intersecting and Parallel Lines
1) $y = 102°$

Page 95 — Geometry Problems
1) $BEF = 100°$

Page 96 — Exterior and Interior Angles
1) Exterior angle = 45°
Interior angle = 135°

Page 97 — Transformations
1) A translation of 2 units right and 7 units down.

Page 98 — Transformations
1) a) & b)

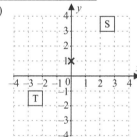

2)

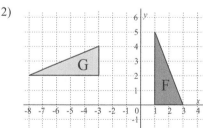

Rotation of 90° (a quarter turn) anticlockwise about point $(-2, -1)$.

Page 99 — Transformations
1)

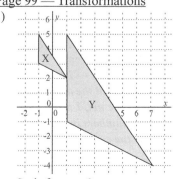

Scale factor = 3

134

Page 100 — Congruent Shapes
1) Yes, because both triangles have interior angles 47° and 98° and a corresponding side of 20 mm, meeting the AAS condition.

Page 101 — Similar Shapes
1) 6 cm

Page 102 — Triangle Construction
1)

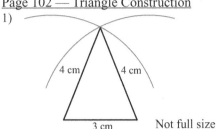

3 cm   Not full size

Page 103 — Pythagoras' Theorem
1) 13 cm

Page 104 — Warm-Up Questions
1) Parallelogram
2) 36 cm^2
3) 3 cm
4) 5
5) 534.1 cm^2 (1 d.p.)
6) 83°
7) Corresponding angles
8)

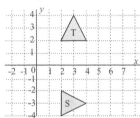

Rotation of 90° clockwise about point (0, 0) or the origin
9) 3
10) If the triangle is right-angled, then $8^2 + 15^2 = 17^2$.
$8^2 + 15^2 = 64 + 225 = 289 = 17^2$, so the triangle is right-angled.

Pages 105-107 — Practice Questions
2) Area of rectangle = 25 × 8 = 200 cm^2
Area of big circle = $\pi R^2 = \pi \times 3^2$
= 28.2743... cm^2
Area of small circle = $\pi r^2 = \pi \times 1.5^2$
= 7.0685... cm^2
Area of shaded region
= 200 – 28.2743... – 7.0685...
= 164.6570... = 164.7 cm^2 (1 d.p.)
[4 marks available — 1 mark for finding the area of the rectangle, 1 mark for finding the area of each circle, 1 mark for the correct answer]
3) Surface area
= 2(5 × 3) + 2(8 × 3) + 2(5 × 8)
= 30 + 48 + 80 = 158 cm^2
[3 marks available — 1 mark for attempting to find the area of each rectangle of the net, 1 mark for putting the numbers in correctly, 1 mark for the correct answer]

4) Exterior angle = 180° – interior angle
= 180° – 150° = 30°
Exterior angle = 360 ÷ n,
so n = 360° ÷ exterior angle.
= 360° ÷ 30° = 12
so the polygon has 12 sides.
[2 marks available — 1 mark for a correct method, 1 mark for the correct answer]
5) E.g. x and GBE are allied angles, so x = 180° – 110° = 70°.
y and GBE are alternate angles, so y = GBE = 110°.
You've just found that y = 110°, so using angles on a straight line, DEC = 180° – 110° = 70°.
Angles in a triangle add up to 180°, so z = 180° – 52° – 70° = 58°.
[4 marks available — 1 mark for attempting to use geometry rules to find missing angles, 1 mark for correct angle x, 1 mark for correct angle y, 1 mark for correct angle z]
Other methods are possible — any sensible method is fine.
6) a) A reflection in the line y = x.
[2 marks available — 1 mark for correct transformation type, 1 mark for the correct equation of the mirror line]
b) Rotation 90° clockwise about (–1, –1)
[3 marks available — 1 mark for correct transformation type, 1 mark for the correct angle, 1 mark for the correct centre of rotation]
7) Volume of a cylinder
= $\pi r^2 h = \pi \times 8^2 \times 40$
= 8042.4771... cm^3 = 8042.5 cm^3
[4 marks available — 1 mark for using the correct formula, 1 mark for substituting the values correctly, 1 mark for attempting to calculate the volume, 1 mark for the correct answer]
8) The vertical side of shape A is 3 squares long. The vertical side of shape B is 6 squares long.
So the scale factor is $\frac{6}{3}$ = 2.

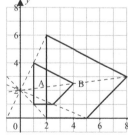

The transformation is an enlargement of scale factor 2 and centre (0, 2).
[3 marks available — 1 mark for correct transformation type, 1 mark for correct scale factor, 1 mark for correct centre of enlargement]

9) Split the triangle in half to give two right-angled triangles:

Use Pythagoras to find the height (x):
$x^2 + 2^2 = 4^2$
$x^2 = 4^2 – 2^2 = 16 – 4 = 12$
$x = \sqrt{12}$ = 3.464... = 3.5 cm (1 d.p.)
[3 marks available — 1 mark for splitting into two right-angled triangles, 1 mark for an attempt to use Pythagoras' theorem, 1 mark for the correct answer]

Page 108 — Summary Questions
1) Lines of symmetry = 2
Order of rotational symmetry = 2
2) E.g. rhombus and parallelogram
3) Octagon
4) Perimeter = 32 cm, area = 55 cm^2
5) 120 cm^2
6) 30 cm^2
7) 201.06 cm^2 (2 d.p.)
8) 22.6 cm^2 (1 d.p.)
9) Faces = 6, edges = 12
10) E.g.

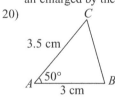

Not full size
Volume = 30 cm^3, surface area = 62 cm^2
11) 48 cm^3
12) a) E.g. 72° (any value above 0° and below 90°)
b) E.g. 111° (any value above 90° and below 180°)
c) E.g. 260° (any value above 180° and below 360°)
13) Alternate angles
14) x = 40°
15) Exterior angle = 36°
Interior angle = 144°
16) (3, 0)
17) (5, 3), (14, 3) and (11, 12)
18) SSS, AAS, SAS, RHS
19) All the angles match up. The sides are all enlarged by the same scale factor.
20)

C
3.5 cm
50°
A   3 cm   B   Not full size
21) 7.14 cm (3 s.f.)
22) 5 (units)

Section 6 — Probability and Statistics

Page 109 — Probability
1) a) 0.1 or $\frac{1}{10}$ b) 0.5 or $\frac{1}{2}$
c) 0.5 or $\frac{1}{2}$

Answers

Page 110 — Probability

1) $\frac{15}{36} = \frac{5}{12}$

(In your table, put the results of adding the scores in the cells.)

2) 12

Page 111 — Experimental Probability

1) Red = 0.43, blue = 0.24, green = 0.33

Page 112 — Data and Tables

1) $\frac{2}{16} = \frac{1}{8}$

Page 113 — Sorting Information

1)
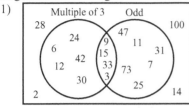

Page 114 — Sorting Information

1)

	Multiple of 5	Not a multiple of 5
Factor of 20	5, 10	1, 2, 4
Not a factor of 20	15	3, 6, 7, 8, 9, 11, 12, 13, 14

Page 115 — Graphs and Charts

1) 4

Page 116 — Graphs and Charts

1)
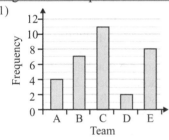

Page 117 — Mean, Median, Mode and Range

1) Median = 11, Mode = 12,
   Mean = 11, Range = 7

Page 118 — Scatter Graphs

1) About 4 years.

Page 119 — Warm-Up Questions

1) a) $\frac{1}{13}$ b) $\frac{1}{4}$ c) $\frac{2}{13}$

2) 8

3) 30

4) 12

5) The bar chart with shoe sizes along the horizontal axis has gaps between bars because the data is discrete.

6) Median = 9, mean = 10

Pages 120-122 — Practice Questions

2) a) First line the data up in order:
   3, 3, 4, 5, 8, 8, 9, 9, 9, 10, 11, 12, 12, 15, 18, 32. The median is halfway between the 8th and 9th values. Median = (9 + 9) ÷ 2 = 9
   [3 marks available — 1 mark for arranging the data in order, 1 mark for finding the position of the middle values, 1 mark for correct answer]

   b) The mode is the most common number: mode = 9 *[1 mark]*

c) Total = 3 + 3 + 4 + 5 + 8 + 8 + 9 + 9 + 9 + 10 + 11 + 12 + 12 + 15 + 18 + 20 + 32 = 168
   Mean = 168 ÷ 16 = 10.5
   [3 marks available — 1 mark for finding the total, 1 mark for calculating the mean, 1 mark for correct answer]

d) Range = 32 − 3 = 29 *[1 mark]*

e) The mean. 32 is significantly higher than any of the other numbers in the data set, so the mean is affected by the extreme value.
   [1 mark for a sensible justification]

3) a) Jayan can't make this assumption because the spinner has only been spun 20 times, so the estimates of the probabilities aren't very accurate *[1 mark]*.

   b) E.g. no, because if it were biased, you would expect the frequency of each colour to vary significantly, but these frequencies are very similar.
   [2 marks available — 1 mark for a comment about either expected frequency or experimental probability, 1 mark for a sensible justification]

4)
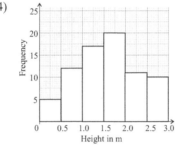
   [3 marks available — 3 marks for all bars drawn correctly, otherwise 2 marks for at least four bars drawn correctly, or 1 mark for at least two bars drawn correctly]

5) Angle of people who play rugby:
   360° − (140° + 80° + 90°) = 50°
   Number of people who play rugby:
   $\frac{50°}{360°} \times 216 = 30$
   [3 marks available — 1 mark for finding the angle for 'rugby', 1 mark for a correct method to calculate the number of people who play rugby, 1 mark for the correct answer]

6) a)
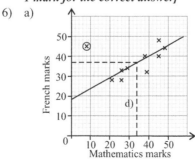
   [3 marks available — 3 marks for all points plotted correctly, otherwise 2 marks for at least six points plotted correctly, or 1 mark for at least three points plotted correctly]

b) E.g. See graph in part a)
   [2 marks available — 1 mark for an appropriate line of best fit, 1 mark for identifying the outlier]

c) Positive correlation *[1 mark]*

d) Go up from 34 on the Mathematics marks axis until you reach the line, then go across to the French marks axis — see graph.
   Expected mark = 37.
   [2 marks available — 1 mark for a correct method, 1 mark for the correct answer]
   Accept any answer between 36 and 38, depending on the line of best fit.

7) Mean = total number of letters ÷ number of students in class
   Total number of letters = 6 × 18 = 108
   Total number of given letters
   = 7 + 3 + 9 + 5 + 4 + 3 + 8 + 6 + 5 + 6 + 4 + 3 + 8 + 10 + 7 + 6 + 8 = 100
   So the missing number is 108 − 100 = 8
   [3 marks available — 1 mark for calculating the total number of letters, 1 mark for a method to find the missing number, 1 mark for the correct answer]

Page 123 — Summary Questions

1) A probability of 1 means that something is certain to happen.

2) $\frac{5}{12}$

3) P(lose) = 0.9

4)
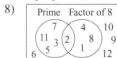

	Second spin	
First spin	Black	White
Black	BB	BW
White	WB	WW

5) Experimental Probability = $\frac{\text{Frequency}}{\text{Number of times you tried}}$

6) Data that can only take countable values.

7) 9 people

8)
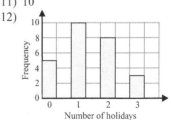

9)

	3 sides	Not 3 sides
All straight sides	C, E	A, F
Not all straight sides	D	B

10) The number of things in each category.

11) 10

12)
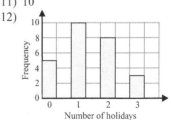

13) Mode = 5, Median = 5,
    Mean = 6, Range = 9

14) 12

15) (Strong) negative correlation

16) 35

Index

MIRT4